# REDEMPTION ROAD

*The Path to Freedom*

CHERISH SADE WHITE

WESTBOW PRESS
A DIVISION OF THOMAS NELSON
& ZONDERVAN

Copyright © 2021 CHERISH SADE WHITE.

All rights reserved. No part of this book may be used or reproduced by any means, graphic, electronic, or mechanical, including photocopying, recording, taping or by any information storage retrieval system without the written permission of the author except in the case of brief quotations embodied in critical articles and reviews.

WestBow Press books may be ordered through booksellers or by contacting:

WestBow Press
A Division of Thomas Nelson & Zondervan
1663 Liberty Drive
Bloomington, IN 47403
www.westbowpress.com
844-714-3454

Because of the dynamic nature of the Internet, any web addresses or links contained in this book may have changed since publication and may no longer be valid. The views expressed in this work are solely those of the author and do not necessarily reflect the views of the publisher, and the publisher hereby disclaims any responsibility for them.

Any people depicted in stock imagery provided by Getty Images are models, and such images are being used for illustrative purposes only. Certain stock imagery © Getty Images.

All Scripture quotations, unless otherwise indicated, are taken from the Holy Bible, New International Version®, NIV®. Copyright ©1973, 1978, 1984, 2011 by Biblica, Inc.® Used by permission of Zondervan. All rights reserved worldwide. www.zondervan.com The "NIV" and "New International Version" are trademarks registered in the United States Patent and Trademark Office by Biblica, Inc.®

Scripture quotations marked (ESV) are from The ESV® Bible (The Holy Bible, English Standard Version®), copyright © 2001 by Crossway, a publishing ministry of Good News Publishers. Used by permission. All rights reserved.

Scripture marked (KJV) taken from the King James Version of the Bible.

Scripture quotations marked (NLT) are taken from the Holy Bible, New Living Translation, copyright ©1996, 2004, 2015 by Tyndale House Foundation. Used by permission of Tyndale House Publishers, Carol Stream, Illinois 60188. All rights reserved.

ISBN: 978-1-6642-1948-9 (sc)
ISBN: 978-1-6642-1949-6 (hc)
ISBN: 978-1-6642-1947-2 (e)

Library of Congress Control Number: 2021901535

Print information available on the last page.

WestBow Press rev. date: 01/28/2021

# CONTENTS

Acknowledgments ..................................................................... vii
Abstract ........................................................................................ ix

Chapter 1   Introduction .......................................................... 1
Chapter 2   My Life .................................................................. 7
Chapter 3   Reentry ................................................................ 11
Chapter 4   The Study Design ............................................... 25
Chapter 5   Biblical Response ............................................... 43
Chapter 6   Integration Factors Affecting Success and Failure .......... 55
Chapter 7   Abstaining from Crime Equals Desistance ...... 71
Chapter 8   Recommendations and Conclusion .................. 79

Bibliography ............................................................................. 85

# ACKNOWLEDGMENTS

*Redemption Road* has been a challenge, and the journey to write it has been long. However, thanks to my Lord and Savior, Jesus Christ, it is complete. Thanks be to God for I can do all things through Christ, who strengthens me. I could have never completed this journey without Him. He is truly the head of my life and the gracious giver of my strength. I never would have made it without Him.

I would like to express my deep appreciation to those who inspired me through this process, namely, the professors of my college. Thank you for your spiritual guidance, patience, dependability, perseverance, and uplifting demeanor throughout it all. As a result of your inspiration, and through your insight and expertise in this area, my eyes have been opened to the many disparities of those impacted by the prison system. Thank you for sharing your experiences and deepening my thirst to take on the project of writing *Redemption Road*.

Another thank-you to the head of my department, who allowed me to put my thoughts into practice during my internship at the seminary I attended. Working with women impacted by incarceration gave me a sense of duty and ministry in the area of women's lives, specifically.

To my husband, son, daughter, and grandchildren: thank you for hanging in there with me. It was a lengthy process, and often I shut myself off from you, but it's finally done! Your help in my work, and in my duties as a mother and grandmother, has not gone unnoticed. I could not have done it without you. Thank you for all your support, morally and emotionally.

Finally, thank you to my mentor and friend, my pastor. You have believed in me even at a time, though it seems like a lifetime ago, when I was one of the women critically affected by reentry into society. You have seen the actual disparities mentioned in *Redemption Road* in my life. Still, you covered me. Today I see that the years the locusts tried to steal have been restored to me. For all of your support, prayers, and words of encouragement, I am truly thankful. Redemption has taken hold of my life, and I am *free*!

\* \* \*

Unless otherwise noted, scripture quotations are taken from the *Holy Bible: New International Version*®. *NIV*®. Copyright © 1973, 1978, 1984 by International Bible Society. Used by permission of Zondervan. All rights reserved.

Scripture quotations designated (*ESV*) are taken from *The Holy Bible, English Standard Version*. Copyright © 2000, 2001 by Crossway Bibles, a division of Good News Publishers. Used by permission. All rights reserved.

Scripture quotations marked "KJV" are taken from the King James Version of the Bible.

Scripture quotations marked (*NLT*) are taken from the *Holy Bible: New Living Translation*, copyright © 1996. Used by permission of Tyndale House Publishers, Inc., Wheaton, IL 60189 USA. All rights reserved.

# ABSTRACT

Throughout history, the prison population has grown exponentially, with women increasingly leading the way in this growth. Despite recent elevation in the prison population, strategies are not being executed to address this societal problem. For women, the problem affects not only their own lives but also the lives of their children and immediate family members. Despite a slight decrease in the overall prison population in recent years, both female offenders and offenders who have breached the conditions of their release are being sent back to prison more frequently. Though there are efforts to create services that provide care continually, the relapse into criminal behavior after women leave the prison system leads to their receiving sanctions or undergoing intervention for a previous crime. Though most studies conducted have focused primarily on male offenders with small samples of women, they have often omitted specifying race as it relates to the ex-offender's release and transition into society. Also left out are the roles of a spiritual foundation in the lives of women and how the church can help bridge the gaps while playing a vital role in the promotion of successful, productive members of society being transitioned from prison.

Reentry introduces variables such as desistance and disparities that are real for female ex-offenders. Therefore, there must be a focus on practical solutions to the challenges faced by women offenders, whether they desist crime or return to criminal behavior. As a community, we must devise and implement strategies to successfully reintegrate women offenders back into the community, along with previously implemented motivating methods that still can be used to desist crime in the lives of women. The question for me became, "How can the community help in bridging the gaps women (with me being the chief ingredient on both ends of the spectrum) experience when transitioning from jails and prisons into society?"

# CHAPTER 1
# INTRODUCTION

The initial thirst for writing *Redemption Road* came while I was working as a PREA volunteer in a federal women's prison subdivision in Charlotte, North Carolina. I became increasingly frustrated watching many offenders be released from the prison and sent to the transition home, only to see them return a short time later. This made me ask, What can be done to eliminate their dilemma when reentering society? The fact was that even women who seemed to have a good chance of successful reentry returned a short time later. Many times I was reluctant to answer calls from the correctional facility because I worried it would be one of my mentees calling to give me news of her being sent back to prison. I began to ponder this phenomenon on a deeper level, instead of simply acknowledging the "revolving door" of the criminal justice system. The answer came as I spoke with those who had left prison and those who were approaching release. They seemed to think that what was happening, in some cases, was that they were being forced to reenter the community when they did not necessarily feel ready for such freedom. Once people leave prison, either when policy and law dictate or when a review board decides to grant, their release, they do not have the tools to survive. Some offenders never go back, whereas others return repeatedly. I looked at the backgrounds and experiences of female offenders who left prison and were supposed to reintegrate into the community while trying to recover in as much detail as possible. My experience of reentry became my primary source of information.

I began doing research on ex-offenders and found Austin and Irwin's mention of the "imprisonment binge" of the last two decades and how it has impacted society and led to an increased number of adults released from prison.[1] According to statistics, nearly seven hundred thousand inmates per year, which is approximately nineteen hundred inmates per day, find themselves being released from prison, whether it be state or federal, and returning home.[2] The vast majority of women sent to prison will inevitably go through the process of leaving prison and returning to society. However, the reentry period opens the door to overwhelming challenges for women, which include finding employment, getting housing, securing treatment, and adhering to the conditions of their parole. More challenges arise as returning prisoners reintegrate into society, which might include the loss of their right to vote, learning how to go about receiving government assistance, educational loans, and professional licenses, and determining whether or not they can hold public office. Women are even more restrained in their reentry as they fight for parental rights or the opportunity even to see their children.

For me, reentry meant either returning to the same environment or being relocated to a halfway house. It meant either being exposed to the same old people, places, and situations that led to my captivity or finding a new way of life. I chose the latter. Despite my having a made-up mind with a set of strategies in place, a trap had been set for me. A restraint I never saw coming was awaiting me in the form of an invisible punishment. These invisible forces were the laws and regulations that had been put in place to do away with my rights and privileges.[3]

Invisible punishments create the vast majority of the disparity experienced by women reentering society. Invisible punishments make it almost impossible for ex-offenders to regain their bearings and get a foothold in society. As a result of not being able to reintegrate back into society or successfully realign themselves with society, women

---

[1] James Austin and John Irwin, *It's about Time: America's Imprisonment Binge* (Belmont, CA: Wadsworth, 2001).
[2] Paige M. Harrison and Allen J. Beck, *Prison and Jail Inmates at Midyear 2005* (Washington, DC: US Department of Justice, Bureau of Justice Statistics, 2006).
[3] Jeremy Travis, *But They All Come Back: Facing the Challenges of Prisoners Reentry* (Washington, DC: Urban Institute Press, 2005).

ex-offenders are more likely to experience recidivism/relapse. According to the national study of recidivism, it is suggested that of the released inmates, two-thirds are rearrested. It also suggests that of the released inmates, 47 percent are reconvicted and about half of them return to prison within a three-year period. The first year following the release of inmates is considered the highest period for recidivism. Of all inmates who are released, 44 percent have been rearrested.[4] Adding to these findings are the statistics related to offenders who have prior offenses, have a history of substance abuse, or have little education. According to statistics, offenders facing reentry with these particular circumstances have been found to recidivate at a greater rate.[5]

In light of these findings regarding the challenges faced by offenders reentering society, I blindly set out to regain my place in the world, but my redemption would not come easily. My first challenge was to acquire housing that would set me up for success, not failure. That meant, for me in particular, not returning to my home. Home for me consisted of my mother, father, children, and siblings. Though I was desperate to regain my place in the lives of my family, I knew full well that I could not return to the same environment that contained the stressors that had caused my knees to buckle and caused me to take flight. I also knew this environment would trigger me in the area of substance abuse. Understand that my family did not indulge me in my substance abuse, nor did they have the dysfunctional issues I possessed before incarceration. My children were looking for a mother, and my family was looking for the person I had been before I became a broken vessel. It was no fault of my family; the responsibility is solely on me. I was the one with the issues, and I had to deal with them head-on.

This is the dilemma for most female ex-offenders reentering society. As mothers, we feel less than adequate when our children are cared for by

---

[4] Patrick A. Langan and David J. Levin, *Recidivism of Prisoners Released in 1994* (Washington, DC: US Department of Justice, Bureau of Justice Statistics, 2002).
[5] Jeffrey T. Ulmer, "Intermediate Sanctions: A Comparative Analysis of the Probability and Severity of Recidivism," *Sociological Inquiry* 71 (2001): 164–93.

others. Often, we feel we the need to make up for lost time or to take back what we had lost during our incarceration. This mentality is one of the greatest enemies to women reentering society. As broken vessels, we need to be healed before we can heal situations we have broken. We need to learn to love ourselves before we can love someone else. We need to forgive ourselves before we can forgive others and move on in life. Until I could get a grasp on my issues, no one but God could mold me back to health in mind, body, and soul.

# CHAPTER 2
# MY LIFE

As the fifth child of a family of eight children, I never wanted for anything. I remember my father working all night and sleeping all day because he was the sole provider for the family. He wanted my mother to be with the children and take care of the house. His example followed me throughout life and kept me seeking a significant other who could fill the shoes he filled for our family. Needless to say, that would be a feat impossible to achieve without the help of God. All my selections were self-made and destructive to my life. I didn't seem to have time to wait on God. My father and mother had brought us up in church and under the tutelage of the Word of God. I remember going to church every Sunday and being there for most of the day. I also recall giving my life to Christ at the age of twelve. It would seem I was secure in my future as a child of my mother and father and even more secure as a child of God. But life had a trap set for me in the form of peer pressure.

Being secure at home under the agape love of my family did not protect me from the wiles of the enemy. Because I was an overachiever destined to excel in school and extracurricular activities, there seemed to be a bull's-eye on my back purposed to destroy me. Throughout my years in elementary and secondary school, I was an honor roll student, often promoted to higher levels of learning. On top of that, I was often at the forefront of any organization I participated in. After receiving numerous awards and enjoying many successes throughout my school years, I was voted most likely to succeed in my senior year of high school. My goal was to become an architect and build new and innovative structures around the country.

The first assault launched against me was in the form of recreational drugs, offered by my peers. Initiating my life of substance abuse, marijuana became a dear friend of mine. As stated by many substance abuse experts, this was the gateway to extreme drug abuse and more crippling substances. I became accustomed to the euphoria and escapism afforded by mind-altering, mood-changing drugs. The studious, well-groomed beauty queen was now on her way to an abyss that would take her to places she had never seen before. I lived to use and used to live.

Such is the case for many ex-offenders. Handling life on life's terms for women can be challenging when life shows up. Whether it shows up in the form of abuse, single parenthood, or other issues, women often attempt to make things better, but those attempts can be the root of their demise. There is no discrimination when it comes to the attacks of the enemy. It does not matter how good you look, your level of education, your family's background, or what your career is; substance abuse and the plethora of issues it introduces often lead to criminal activity that lands women in the judicial system. As for me, my last year of college was interrupted by my first trip to county jail for possession of marijuana. This was the beginning of twenty years of despair and the end of my dreams of success, which were now dreams deferred. My attempts to break free from the vicious cycle of reentry into jail were exasperated time and time again because I did not know how to stay free. Once I picked up drugs again, I was back behind bars. It was made clear to me after repeated trips to county jail that I was allergic to drugs; they always made me "break out in handcuffs." It was not until my first and only trip to prison that I knew something was desperately wrong and that I needed help. My actions were affecting not only me but also my two children of one and three years of age. They were being robbed of the life I had been so freely given by my parents. The desire to stay clean and free was so strong, but the desire for drugs always won out. This dilemma needed an answer I could not give, so I turned it over to God and sought redemption.

# CHAPTER 3
# Reentry

Many scholars have attempted to examine the complex issues associated with the disparities of women and their reentry into society from prison. As mentioned earlier, trying to take possession of life after prison is not an easy task. It involves elements such as finding a job, obtaining a place to reside, getting formal documents such as identification, and becoming connected and reunited with members of one's family. Adding to these issues is the need to change old playgrounds and old playmates as women often transition to or reenter the same type of environment from which they came before prison. There is also the need to address substance abuse and substance dependence, as well as to steer clear of criminal activity. One of the major issues is securing a job. Often women offenders have a sporadic work history, which is now coupled with a criminal record.[6] With the rise in the number of women inhabiting the criminal justice system comes the need to be more attentive to distinctly different strategies to divert them from crime and courts and to offer support that addresses the disparities and risk factors they face that push them into becoming repeat offenders.

When comparing the study of gender in terms of reentry into society, far less is known about women than about men offenders who regain their freedom. A study conducted by Harrison and Beck revealed that imprisonment for women is growing at a faster rate than the rate for men.[7] Thus, capturing how to address positive reentry strategies is a must given the expectation of the rise in the number of women returning

---

[6] Christy A. Visher and Jeremy Travis, "Transition from Prison to Community: Understanding Individual Pathways," *Annual Review of Sociology* 29 (2003): 89–113.
[7] Paige M. Harrison and Allen J. Beck, *Prison and Jail Inmates at Midyear 2005* (Washington, DC: US Department of Justice, Bureau of Justice Statistics, 2006).

home. Though the challenges are similar for most inmates exiting prison, this qualitative study shows that the disparities faced during the reentry experiences of women are different from those of their male counterparts. The most compelling finding in the study showed that men often return to a home and a family.[8] They are also more likely to secure a job that generates income.[9] For the female ex-offender, this oftentimes means securing employment that offers income sufficient enough to allow her to care for her children and herself. As a result of not finding this income, many women need supplemental income in the form of social services. This becomes a paradoxical situation. It was one from which I could not escape because of contradictory rules or the limitations placed on me because I was an ex-offender. Policies and government stipulations often deny assistance to women who have been convicted of felony or federal offenses. The complex issues faced by women reentering society are unequal in their degree and are distinctly different for women than for men. This creates the disparities for women who reenter society. It has been proven to be very difficult for the average woman who leaves prison who "lacks a home, financial support, employment, socially legitimated and rewarded skills, practical knowledge about how to secure resources, and most of all, lack of a sense of hope for their future outside of prison."[10]

No matter my educational level or all the successes I had experienced in life, after I had been charged with a felony, I had difficulty finding employment upon my release. It was only by the grace of God that I was hired by a church member who had known me before my downward spiral toward destruction. I worked for him doing body work on cars. This was a far cry from my dreams of being an architect. My education was in the field of mechanical engineering, but life had robbed me of the opportunity to work in that field. My work history was damaged

---

[8] Joanne Belknap, *The Invisible Woman: Gender, Crime, and Justice* (Belmont, CA: Wadsworth, 1996).
[9] Patricia O'Brien, *Making It in the "Free World": Women in Transition from Prison* (Albany: State University of New York Press, 2001).
[10] Ibid., 2–3.

by sporadic and short-term jobs that I had fit around my addiction. Returning to society left me feeling hopeless as a productive worker because I was not doing what I had studied for years to do. This deep feeling of failure kept me locked in an unfulfilled life that led me back to drug use. Needless to say, I returned to jail with another notch in my belt, stamped "Relapse." Drugs always led me to criminal behavior, but mine, I felt, was not as severe as that of the next female offender. After all, I was only hurting myself. I would soon find that the hurt I had inflicted was not just on me but also on my family, my children, and my God, who I now believe grieved each time I fell short.

It becomes plain to see that many women leaving prison face barriers that are invincible. Reflective of these barriers is the amount of women who have successive contact with the criminal justice system. According to a recent cross-state estimate of recidivism, 58 percent of incarcerated women experience rearrest with 38 percent of these women being reconvicted. Of this number, 30 percent are returned to prison within three years of their release.[11] Thus, the argument of many feminists becomes a matter of victimization when discussing female criminality and recidivism/relapse. There are those who also argue that victimization happened long before prison for the female offender in the form of physical and sexual abuse.[12] Others suggest that continued victimization in childhood and adulthood is linked to continued criminal offenses among women.[13]

The barriers for me involved some of those explored by experts. Physical abuse began for me with my first husband and continued for eleven years. After losing two children at the hands of my first husband, I began

---

[11] Elizabeth P. Deschenes, Barbara Owen, and Jason Crow, *Recidivism among Female Prisoners: Secondary Analysis of the 1994 BJS Recidivism Data Set, Final Report* (Washington, DC: National Institute of Justice, 2007).

[12] Lawrence A. Greenfeld and Tracy L. Snell, *Women Offenders* (Washington, DC: Bureau of Justice Statistics, 1999).

[13] Meda Chesney-Lind, "Imprisoning Women: The Unintended Victims of Mass Imprisonment, in *Invisible Punishment: The Collateral Consequences of Mass Imprisonment*, edited by Marc Mauer and Meda Chesney-Lind (New York: New Press, 2002).

to seek a way to break free from his abuse when I became pregnant a third time. During our marriage, I returned to school, seeking my bachelor's degree, which I had put on hold because of my substance abuse. I tried desperately to get a grip on my life and regain my dreams. But my choice in a spouse totally hindered my success in this area. His possessiveness and jealousy kept me enslaved to living outside the will of God. I had made the choice, and now I was living with the consequences. Finally, upon delivery of a healthy baby boy, the nightmare of losing two children was lifted. I finally felt like a woman worthy of having a child. Imbedded in me were the spiritual principles my parents, along with my church, had taught me. I fought hard to stay clean and be a good mother and wife. I fought hard to change my husband because I saw some good in him. I fought hard to live the dream I had envisioned as a child.

However, after the delivery of my son, the abuse started again. It did not start over, but it picked up where it left off. The slapping became punches, the pushing became knockdowns, the holding became choking, and the hitting became kicking. The abuse became a norm for me because, in my twisted mind with its twisted vision of love, I believed my husband loved me so much that he abused me. It was not until I met a couple in San Antonio, Texas, that I realized abuse is not love. In fact, it is the opposite of love. So, with my baby in my arms, one day I decided to flee and return home to North Carolina. I had no clothes or possessions, but I sat in the airport with my son and the couple God had put in my life to save me. Upon arrival in North Carolina, I had a welcome committee of family waiting with open arms. Still, I sought comfort from my old friend, drugs. I didn't know how to take away the pain of the abuse or the pain of a failed marriage. I didn't know how to regain my confidence and my dreams. I was lost, even though I finally felt safe. Drugs, again, became my escape mechanism.

Shortly after I'd arrived in North Carolina, my husband reached out to me and demanded that I return with his son. When I denied his request, he came to me from Texas. Once again, my twisted idea of love led me back into a spiral of marital uncertainty. My life hinged on my husband's move to be with me and his son. I felt he really loved me and would change in this environment. Needless to say, this geographical change did not change him or me. Both of us began to use drugs in a way that took control of our lives. Being constantly high, coupled with intermediate abuse and neglect, became our way of life. The stories associated with this lifestyle are too many to put on paper. Thus, summarizing them all makes up a picture of life of two people desperately enabling each other in total dysfunction.

Things began to change (after losing my first two children and now having a beautiful baby boy) with the pregnancy of my fourth child. I stopped the substance abuse and enrolled in college to complete my last year of mechanical engineering. I was determined to be all that I could be once again. During a visit to my doctor for a routine appointment, it was revealed that the baby was in distress. I was suffering from placenta previa and would have to be on complete bed rest for the remainder of the pregnancy. Because I was hospitalized for three months with my fourth child, I completed my semester in the hospital with professors retrieving my assignments in person. While I had set out to make a change, my husband was still sunk in hopeless addiction.

My fourth and last child was born healthy, while I lay fighting for my life. This pregnancy left me unable to have any other children and on the brink of death. For ten days I fought for my life while my daughter went home with my mother. On the day my eyes opened, I knew life would never be the same. That didn't mean I wouldn't see the enemy again in the form of substance abuse and incarceration, but it did mean that I realized God had a plan for my life that no enemy could stop. It was up to me to reach my destiny.

Fast-forward to my reunion with my husband, which brought me to pick up drugs again after having been clean for over a year. Again, things got so bad that my husband and I decided to pack up and drive over twelve hundred miles to Texas. We slept in the car with two babies, eighteen months and three months of age. When we arrived, we stayed with family. The dysfunction of it all kept me feeling empty, hopeless, helpless, and unfulfilled. Once again the physical abuse started, but this time I had had enough. Never had I called the police on my husband. Never had his hands missed my face and hit my three-month-old baby. Never had he used my eighteen-month-old child as a tool to keep me with him. As I watched him from behind a door, dragging my son down the street with his little legs trying to keep up, I knew this was it! I called the police and found myself standing in the presence of two female Hispanic officers five minutes later. Their determination to help me find my son led to his return within an hour. From that moment on, I began to plan my permanent departure from my husband.

The fact that I had called the police was utterly unacceptable to my husband. The next day, he went in full force with the abuse. I had to run for my life, leaving my children with his family. Once I got to a phone, I felt the back of my head and knew I had been injured physically like never before. I called the local assistance program, which put me in touch with a battered women's shelter. I was picked up and taken to a safe haven, but my heart was broken as I cried desperately for my children. Allowed to use the phone, I called my sister-in-law to ask that she and/or my brother bring my children to me. Despite her displeasure with my decision, she brought them to me. Now came the tedious task of calling my mother to send someone to collect me. This would be the third time she had done so, but I knew of nowhere else to turn. She told me that she would not send for me, adding that I was the one who had made the choice to be with my husband. I was devastated. Seeing the despair on my face, the director of the shelter, I later found out, had called my mom back and told her of the seriousness of my situation. Once again my mom sent for me, but this time I would have to travel twenty-three hours on a bus with two babies without diapers, food, or clothes. We boarded the bus, never to see this life again.

As the breadwinner and sole provider for my children, I now knew I must survive and make a change, not for me, but for my children. Never before had I felt so desperate to change! I had just witnessed the father of my children hit my three-month-old daughter; all the love I had had for him went out the window at that moment. Now, after traveling twenty-three hours on a bus with my babies, I was home. I never went back. The dreams I had of being affluent and prosperous were now very dim, but I was determined to do whatever was necessary to provide for my children and myself. This meant government assistance, something I felt I would never accept. However, once settling down at home, I acquired assistance and began to reach for my dreams once again. I enrolled in college and began trying to complete my degree. But that old habit kept calling me to escape the thoughts of failure I had experienced throughout my life. Without my having accepted in my mind the redemption work of God, I gave in to the drugs once again. This left me struggling to provide for my family while supporting my habit of drug addiction. The fight was heated as I walked through moments of clarity to stay clean and lived in prison as an addict. I was forced to move in with my mother and live below the standards God had for me. I cried out to God many times to loose me, to set me free, to deliver me from myself. I never thought, with all I had accomplished in life, that I would live in lack and depend on others to fix my poverty. It seemed the attack on my life by way of drug addiction and poverty was meant to destroy me, and it almost did. But God!

There is additional empirical evidence reflecting that the poverty status of women exiting prison and reentering society strongly increases the odds of rearrest in the female felony offender community.[14] Findings in this study by Holtfreter and his colleagues reveal that those women who receive financial support through government assistance are less likely to become repeat offenders. Studies also conclude that black women are affected at a higher rate because of their status in society. Unlike her female counterpart, the black woman becomes a victim of economic marginalization and structural dislocation. In one of these studies, black women were highlighted as suffering from economic hopelessness

---

[14] Kristy L. Holtfreter, Michael D. Reisig, and Merry Morash, "Poverty, State Capital, and Recidivism among Women Offenders," *Criminology and Public Policy* 3 (2004): 185–208.

stemming from their lack of legitimate income-generating options and their limitations based on racism, classism, and sexism.[15] According to additional studies, marginalized women who face a worsening economic situation in society are directly related to increased rates of women's offending.[16]

> The most recent correctional census indicates that more than 1.3 million women are under the control of the criminal justice system in the United States. Approximately 213,000 women are in correctional institutions and 1.1 million are under community supervision. As of 2007, 114,000 women (7 percent of all those sentenced to state and federal prisons) were in prison.[17] As of midyear 2008, more than 99,000 women (12 percent of the total jail population) were confined in local jails and detention centers.[18] Women represent 24 percent of the 4.2 million people on probation and 12 percent of the 798,000 people on parole. Although the overall growth of prison admissions slowed in 2007 (a 0.2-percent increase versus a 2.6-percent average annual increase from 2000 to 2007), the number of women incarcerated and supervised by the criminal justice

---

[15] Llad Phillips and Harold L. Votey, "Black Women, Economic Disadvantage, and Incentive to Crime," *American Economic Association Papers and Proceedings* 74 (1984): 293–97.

[16] Karen Heimer, "Changes in the Gender Gap in Crime and Women's Economic Marginalization," in *Criminal Justice 2000: The Nature of Crime, Continuity, and Change*, edited by Gary LaFree, vol. 1 (Washington, DC: National Institute of Justice, 2000).

[17] H. C. West and W. J. Sabol, *Prison Inmates at Midyear 2008—Statistical Tables* (Washington, DC: US Department of Justice, Office of Justice Programs, Bureau of Justice Statistics, 2009).

[18] T. D. Minton and W. J. Sabol, *Jail Inmates at Midyear 2008—Statistical Tables* (Washington, DC: US Department of Justice, Office of Justice Programs, Bureau of Justice Statistics, 2009).

system has maintained a sharp upward trajectory since 1995, outpacing that of male offenders.[19]

## The Contribution of Substance Abuse and Family Structure

Studies go on to highlight an overwhelming contributor to the disparities of females exiting the prison system. Brought to light is the issue of substance abuse and its contribution to the disparities among females exiting prison. It is critical to understand how substance abuse affects the success of women reentering society. It is listed in studies as one of the most common reasons for recidivism/relapse.[20] For many females, coping with life on life's terms is not easy. Adding to this dilemma are the barriers faced when reentering society and seeking freedom, not only from prison, but also from mental, physical, and emotional pain. Studies show that women use drugs as a coping mechanism and often seek them for relief of the pain of abuse. Some resort to the sale of drugs as a means of supporting themselves and their children.[21] This practice among female ex-offenders often leads them to the illegal drug market, whether it is for consumption or for financial support. This in turn opens the door to the possibility of being rearrested and convicted of felony charges. The likelihood of becoming an ex-offender serving time once again is immensely probable given the seriousness of the crime and the likelihood of the woman's being already on parole.

Still other studies present the family structure as an empirical factor that shapes successful postrelease for women. According to scholarly experiments and observation, although marital status and job

---

[19] L. E. Glaze, and T. P. Bonczar, *Probation and Parole in the United States, 2006* (Washington, DC: US Department of Justice, Office of Justice Programs, Bureau of Justice Statistics, 2007).

[20] Kamala Mallik-Kane and Christy A. Visher, *Health and Prisoner Reentry: How Physical, Mental, and Substance Abuse Conditions Shape the Process of Reintegration* (Washington, DC: Urban Institute, 2008).

[21] Kathleen Daly, "Gender, Crime, and Criminology," in *The Handbook of Crime and Justice*, edited by Michael Tonry (Oxford: Oxford University Press, 1998).

stability come through as factors in the successful reentry into society among males, the disparity or difference in the case of females is insurmountable.[22] For women, relationships are more emotionally based than for men. Thus, strong relationships bring about positive effects for women. Studies conducted revealed that children catapult women and serve as change agents for them.[23] This evidence suggests that in order to understand the disparities of women, ensure that they successfully engage in their reentry process, and alleviate recidivism, family and parental relationships must be evaluated and deemed essential.

It is necessary for me to express that after years of substance abuse, physical abuse, and repeated incarceration, I was set free by God. Though I lost many years and suffered needless pain, once I took the matter to God and left it there, He showed me strategies and steps to take to get free and stay free. No more relapse, no more recidivism, no more enslavement, no more needless pain. I had learned not only to desist crime but also to desist the repeated relapse that always led to my incarceration.

## The Theory of Desistance

Some might suggest that the current studies are unable to truly understand why the disparities for women cause such a dilemma in their lives. However, the theory of desistance from crime, which is long-term abstinence from criminal behavior among those for whom offending has become a pattern of behavior, is somewhat puzzling. Theories have been developed that seek to produce or encourage desistance and that are the express focus of much criminal justice policy, practice, and research. Interventions have been designed to reduce the disparities

---

[22] Peggy C. Giordano, Stephen A. Cernkovich, and Jennifer L. Rudolph, "Gender, Crime, and Desistance: Toward a Theory of Cognitive Transformation," *American Journal of Society* 107 (2002): 990–1064.

[23] Trina L. Hope, Esther I. Wilder, and Toni T. Watt, "The Relationships among Adolescent Pregnancy, Pregnancy Resolution, and Juvenile Delinquency," *Sociological Quarterly* 44 (2003): 555–76.

of women exiting prison, along with justice interventions that are designed to measure the effectiveness of the desistance theory. There is little agreement on the definition of desistance or on the measure of desistance from crime.

The following is according to Laub and Sampson:

> Termination is the time at which criminal activity stops. Desistance, by contrast, is the causal process that supports the termination of offending. While it is difficult to ascertain when the process of desistance begins, it is apparent that it continues after the termination of offending. In our view, the process of desistance maintains the continued state of nonoffending. Thus, both termination and the process of desistance need to be considered in understanding cessation from offending. By using different terms for these distinct phenomena, we separate termination (the outcome) from the dynamics underlying the process of desistance (the cause), which have been confounded in the literature to date.[24]

While some term desistance as permanently ceasing criminal activity for several years, others argue a less fixed definition of desistance. Those who argue this latter point accept the idea that episodes of reoffending may occur. Thus, the ambiguity associated with the definition has raised debate in research literature as to how desistance is measured. This leads to additional debates on how to use the information and insight derived from the study of desistance. The goal of the criminal justice system is to reduce crime. Therefore, understanding the how and why of desistance in women ex-offenders is vitally important. It allows the gaps to be filled

---

[24] John H. Laub and Robert J. Sampson, "Understanding Desistence from Crime," *Crime and Justice* 28 (2001): 1–69.

in the area of knowledge about criminal careers. It also provides insight that is useful for policy makers and criminal justice agencies.

Despite the findings of research related to the validity of crime and desistance, the dynamics of the study associated with women is noticeably absent from the literature. Therefore, I conducted an examination of whether these theories are applicable to women offenders by interviewing women exiting correctional facilities in North Carolina. These facilities house female inmates of all custody levels and control statuses, including death row, maximum security, close custody, medium security, minimum security, and safekeepers. The women interviewed included recently released individuals living under prison mandates but transitioning to reentry by living at transitional homes. The homes are residential facilities for women who are still incarcerated and serving out the final years of their prison sentences. The interviews also included women who had been transitioned from transitional homes into the community. The amount of time of their reentry ranged from two months to four years. Because desistance is an ongoing process, the women interviewed were ex-offenders who were actively working daily to remain crime-free. Whether they were buying into socially accepted goals as a means to achieve them, or whether the threat or perceived threat of punishment was the key to their desistance, I found that studying this theory and its process and assisting offenders to go through the process reflected that this theory would bring about the greatest reduction in offending.[25] This reduction would require understanding that the reasons why women offenders stop their criminal behavior is different from the process of going straight and maintaining desistance.[26] The desisting sample of women had initiated and sustained their continued crime-free behavior for a two-to-three-year period, making it possible to understand the process of desistance and how the disparities of women can be overcome systematically.

---

[25] Laub, "Understanding Desistance from Crime."
[26] Shadd Maruna, *Making Good: How Ex-Convicts Reform and Rebuild Their Lives* (Washington, DC: American Psychological Association, 2001).

# CHAPTER 4
# THE STUDY DESIGN

Close examination of twenty-eight women housed at one of these transitional homes allowed me to conduct a systematic analysis of two groups of offenders. The groups were made up of (1) those who had been recently released from a state prison and were residing in a transitional home, awaiting transition from the transitional home to complete freedom, and (2) those who had been released on parole from the transitional home and who were now living on the outside. Upon interviewing these female ex-offenders, I examined the similarities and differences in their process of desistance and the disparities they faced. Also, the accounts of their life experiences helped to determine why some desist from crime during different phases of reentry and why some do not. According to Miller, research that offers comparative strategies can be useful for fortifying "internal validity by allowing for more refined analysis and greater contextual specification."[27] Utilizing this concept, I structured the interviews to determine the factors related to the ex-offenders' disparities and then made a direct correlation between their desistance and recidivism.

The sampling strategy used also explored the manner in which women handled their release from prison. It also examined the disparities that contributed to their offenses and the factors contributing to their postrelease success. Thus, the methods and resources used to achieve reentry into the community are integral elements of desistance. When conducting this sampling strategy, I found it important to select a time frame that would provide an accurate view of the postrelease period. The time frame of incarceration varied for each ex-offender; however,

---

[27] Jody Miller, "The Status of Qualitative Research in Criminology" (paper presented at the National Science Foundation Workshop on Interdisciplinary Standards for Systematic Qualitative Research, Washington, DC, 2005).

each ex-offender had to have less than two years left on her sentence if transitioning into the transitional home. The first group was comprised of women still residing at the transitional home, while the second group was comprised of women who had left the transitional home and were now integrated into society. Though the number in each group was different, they present an approximately equal criterion for the study. The women studied had no additional crimes or violations, nor had they been returned to the state prison from which they had come.

The reason I chose the transitional home was because of its connection with the state prison that had formerly housed the transitioning ex-offenders. As the primary Department of Public Safety prison facility, the state prison houses female inmates on a thirty-acre campus. It is the primary support facility for the six other women's prisons throughout the state. The population is the largest in the state, and it consists of women inmates of all custody levels and control statuses. As mentioned before, this includes death row, maximum security, close custody, medium security, minimum security, and safekeepers. The transitional home was chosen because it is the transitional stage for women leaving the state prison and reentering society. The transitional home is a nonprofit organization that has as its goal to build the community and strengthen those who have criminal records to desist from crime. Not only does the transitional home provide resources and services to assist women ex-offenders, but also it aids women who have been released from incarceration, as well as their families. Because of alarming statistics, the transitional home decided to take on the task of building people, not prisons. Some of the statistics that motivated the vision of the transitional home are as follows:

- Federal and state correctional facilities held over 1.6 million prisoners at the end of 2010—approximately one in every 201 US residents.
- At least 95 percent of state prisoners will be released and sent back to their communities at some point.

- During 2010, 708,677 sentenced prisoners were released from state and federal prisons, an increase of nearly 20 percent from 2000.
- Approximately nine million individuals are released from jail each year.
- Nearly 4.9 million individuals were on probation or parole at the end of 2010.
- In a study that looked at recidivism in over forty states, more than four in ten offenders returned to state prison within three years of their release.
- In 2009, parole violators accounted for 33.1 percent of all prison admissions, 35.2 percent of state admissions, and 8.2 percent of federal admissions.
- Twenty-three percent of adults exiting parole in 2010—127,918 individuals—returned to prison as a result of violating their terms of supervision. Nine percent of adults exiting parole in 2010—49,334 individuals—returned to prison as a result of a new conviction.[28]

Though the transitional home with a thirty-bed capacity is essential to the desistance of the female ex-offender, there is more. Incorporated in the transitional home is the work-release program, which guides women into productive living and independence. There is also a program known as Lifeworks, a stable program that has the longest success rate of the transitional home. Its main focus is navigating women with criminal records into the mainstream of employment by helping them to obtain and retain jobs. Last but not least is the program known as Families Doing Time, which was originated as, and operates as, a source for strengthening families. Its goal is to provide the incarcerated female and her family tools to stop the cycle of intergenerational incarceration.

Still today, women make up the fastest-growing portion of the prison and jail populations. The number of females incarcerated has increased

---

[28] Center for Community Transition, http://www.centerforcommunitytransitions.org/.

by 50 percent since 1995. As of December, 2003, 101,179 women were being held in state or federal prisons. This represents 6.9 percent of the total prison population.[29] However, the dynamics of the typical female prisoner have changed in that there is an increasingly large number of minorities incarcerated. Female inmates also are depicted as being older than in previous years, while continuing to be undereducated and underemployed before incarceration. Lastly, two distinct dynamics have been revealed: (1) 80 percent of women in prison are mothers of young children, and (2) an increasingly large number of incarcerated women have survived sexual and/or physical violence perpetrated by a male relative or significant other.[30] Thus, the first characteristic of the women interviewed in the sample was that those transitioning from the state prison and residing in the transitional home awaiting transition (Group 1) were attempting to reconnect with their children and families. However, given their desire to make up for lost time, they suffered from guilt and shame, as well as inadequacy in the area of providing for their children. This disparity draws on the fact that living in the transitional home requires working at select jobs for which offer ex-offenders had little opportunity. The rules of the house require women to work only in certain areas of the community, performing only certain duties, and being classified at a specific employment status with the company providing employment. This restriction minimizes the potential to secure employment in areas where the ex-offender is qualified. There is also the restriction of using only public transportation. This limits the distance and the locales of jobs for the women ex-offenders. The limitations often lift the desire to desist from crime despite the parameters and regulations of the transitional home.

Adding to this dilemma is the limited contact with children and families because of state and government stipulations. If one ex-offender commits a violation in the transitional home, generally all the residents suffer

---

[29] P. M. Harrison and A. J. Beck, *Prisoners in 2003: Bureau of Justice Statistics Report* (Washington, DC: US Department of Justice, 2004).
[30] Ibid.

the consequences. The privilege to receive visitors is taken away, along with privileges asserted in the home. Once again, the desire to desist is surmounted by the quenching effect of being a "law-abiding resident" who reaps no benefit for her desistance from additional offenses. Though this may not be the case for Group 2, when comparing the characteristics of the two groups in the sample, I found that the distribution across each group revealed family income and single female parent similarities. It also revealed similarities in poverty levels and unemployment. For those women interviewed in Group 2, it was found that they were worse off at times because of the neighborhoods they were residing in and the housing afforded to them given their economic status. This status is directly related to sporadic job history and criminal record. Another barrier that reflected a disparity was the median income of ex-offenders. It is more than $15,000 lower for the neighborhoods where respondents are living, and the number of African Americans living at this level of poverty is more than double compared to others.[31] The two groups sampled in the interviews expressed deep concern for their future economic conditions as well as concern for their ability to desist from crime given the disparities they faced. This led to a conversation with each of the women, in hopes of revealing some of the pitfalls they felt a were threat to their success. By knowing the background of the sampled women, I was able to lead the conversation with open-ended questions that made mention of the similarities found in statistics and in their interviews. The questions included details about the onset of their criminal behavior, their drug use, their time spent in prison, and their prerelease and postrelease challenges. According to Bloom, Owen, and Covington, it was found that alcohol and other drugs are used by women to "self-medicate" and that "property and drug crimes can be conceptualized as survival crimes and have been tied to economic and emotional struggles."[32] Under these circumstances, the transitional

---

[31] Ibid.

[32] Barbara Bloom, Barbara Owen, and Stephanie Covington, *Gender-Responsive Strategies for Women Offenders: A Summary of Research, Practice, and Guiding Principles for Women Offenders* (Washington, DC: US Department of Justice, National Institute of Corrections, NIC Accession Number 020418, 2005).

home, the state prison, and other correctional and community resources should strategically target the economic and personal survival needs of women.[33]

## Sampling

Barriers presented by the disparities among female ex-offenders were a challenge to explore. In order to examine the issues blocking successful desistance of female ex-offenders, I had to use practical and adequate tactics. Thus, a purposive sampling strategy was utilized to explore the issues of the sampling group to determine how women adjust to and maintain their freedom after their release from prison, as well as to discover the factors contributing to their participation in crime. Evidence of the methods and resources that can be used to facilitate reintegration into the community can then be employed to achieve greater desistance, leading to a bridge in the gap of the disparities. When comparing the characteristics of the sample, I found that one of the greatest challenges facing female offenders is in the area of employment. The majority of female offenders are economically dismissed and face considerable challenges upon their reentry into the community after incarceration.[34] As a result of these challenges, efforts to obtain and maintain employment are impeded.

All the women in the sample group expressed these disparities and recognized the challenges they would face upon reentering the community. As a distinct community within society, female ex-offenders are not only underemployed but also unemployed, and if employed, making less per hour than their male counterparts. They are also subject to taking temporary jobs and being placed into lower-level

---

[33] E. P. Deschenes, Barbara Owen, and J. Crow, *Recidivism among Female Prisoners: Secondary Analysis of the 1994 BJS Recidivism Data Set* (Washington, DC: US Department of Justice, Office of Justice Programs, National Institute of Justice, 2007).

[34] R. Zarch and G. Schneider, *The Jewish Vocational Services Women Offender Reentry Collaborative—A Practitioner's "Blueprint" for Replication* (Cambridge, MA: Abt Associates, 2007).

or entry-level positions that offer minimal chances for advancement.[35] There were, however, two discrepancies in the sample group. The first discrepancy was the ratio of African American respondents to Caucasian respondents. Of the twenty-eight women, seventeen were African American and eleven were Caucasian. The second discrepancy lay in the types of offenses committed by the respondents. Though their crimes were not known to me because of confidentially matters, it was evident that they were model inmates as reflected in their privilege to have been transitioned to the transitional home. This, then, does not reflect the population of those still housed in the state prison, where there is no representation of the prison and parole populations.

## Methodology

Before interviewing each respondent, I briefed them on the study. I also discussed their rights and carefully reviewed the guidelines for the transitional home. They all signed papers acknowledging their informed consent; these went to the appropriate department of the state prison. I was trained on their rights and the conduct expected of me as a state prison sponsor/mentor/volunteer, and underwent an extensive background check. I was also informed of my rights as a participant and active correspondent with the female ex-offenders. I was unable to interview every woman coming in or leaving the transitional home because of the turnover rate of women leaving on their release dates and others coming in to fill their slots. Of the women in the home during the period of time I was doing my research, there were a total of forty-five who could have been interviewed. Though all forty-five met the criteria for sampling, not all of them wanted to participate. Of the forty-five, ten did not want to participate, two had had their parole revoked, one was sent to the hospital after having been hit by a car on the way to work, and five had entered the transitional home too late to add credence to

---

[35] C. L. Blitz, "Predictors of Stable Employment among Female Inmates in New Jersey: Implications for Successful Reintegration," *Journal of Offender Rehabilitation* 43, no. 1 (2006): 1–22.

the survey. The names of the respondents are not included in the project for confidentiality/privacy reasons.

The total number of women selected and interviewed was twenty-eight. Of the twenty-eight women interviewed, twelve had successfully completed their stays at the transitional home and had completely transitioned into the community. The remaining sixteen women of the sampling survey included six who had been sent back and ten who were coming up on their release dates from the transitional home, moving toward reentry into the community. My desire to interview this diverse sample of female ex-offenders and follow their progress was coupled with my desire to match the two groups as closely as I could. I purposefully matched the samples using the factors and variables directly related to recidivism and desistance. The variables used in the correlation reflect the barriers to crime and their effects on the disparities of female ex-offenders.

An interesting similarity was found during the study revealing that age, the number of times incarcerated, and marital status were evenly sprawled. Within my study, however, there were other discrepancies found, such as the number of women in the sample groups who were of African American descent and the number who were of Caucasian decent. There were almost two times the number of African American women in my parole sample than Caucasian women, as compared to the parole population within the state, which lists that African American women are incarcerated at three times the rate of Caucasian women. For the purposes of this project, I had to incorporate an operational approach using the strengths of the method chosen: interviews. Since desistance and disparities were the variables being looked at, it was important to highlight the outcomes and effects on the sample group. There are scholars who rely on official criminal records as a source to measure desistance. This is done by looking at the change over a period of time, arrest, conviction, and incarceration.[36] Also, because policies and law enforcement practices tend to reflect inaccurate measurements in crime given bias among police and errors in reporting crime, the limitations of research done by law enforcement agencies and their policies were taken into account when approaching this project. Another method used for measuring variables is the survey. This methodology is common and serves as a great contribution to the study of large populations; however, it requires self-reports on crime.[37] Still another methodology is rooted in direct interviews. When looking at the disparities and desistance of female ex-offenders, it is important not to generalize the finding, but to paint a picture from the perspective of the participants/respondents. Thus, to get a bird's-eye view on the case in hand, I used the interview/narrative methodology in this project to measure desistance.[38] Maruna shares that this type of methodology offers in-depth detail about the process of desistance from the perspective of the interviewee. In this project, the use of narratives or interviews allowed the female ex-offenders the opportunity to share a conversation, in their own words, about their own perceptions of their desistance and how they moved away from crime. Because my sample was small, consisting of twenty-eight women, this methodology provided a qualitative study that offers findings that are not generalizable outside the bounds of the interview sample.

## Limitations

For the project, limitations had to be considered when using this operational approach. With this in mind, both official measurements and subjective measurements were used to examine desistance. It was

---

[36] Christy A. Visher, Pamela K. Lattimore, and Richard L. Linster, "Predicting the Recidivism of Serious Youthful Offenders Using Survival Models," *Criminology* 29 (1991): 329–66.

[37] Michael Massoglia and Christopher Uggen, "Subjective Desistance and the Transition to Adulthood," *Journal of Contemporary Criminal Justice* 23 (2007): 90–103.

[38] John H. Laub and Robert J. Sampson, *Shared Beginnings, Divergent Lives: Delinquent Boys to Age 70* (Cambridge, MA: Harvard University Press, 2003).

necessary to use the same approach to look at the disparities that hinder desistance when attempting to reenter the community as a female ex-offender. However, the primary task was to determine how the women overcame the disparities in order to gain knowledge regarding their desistance from crime. The gauge or benchmark for measuring desistance was the actual action of not returning to prison for a period of two to three years after release. This measuring benchmark is a direct result of *not* committing a new offense or enacting a technical violation over the allotted two-to-three-year period. Using two to three years as a time frame offered the objective approach to the study given the fact that long-term follow-up studies approximate that the recidivism rate of female ex-offenders within a three-year period is two-thirds of that of those released from prison. This suggests that approximately two-thirds of offenders recidivate within three years of their release from prison.[39]

It was now time to establish the subjective approach to the sample in order to offer inclusion of the interview/narratives. Thus, the participants provided me with self-reports about noncriminal participation since their release from prison. This would mean they were desisting crime and had used the tools/resources afforded them to meet the disparities of reentry successfully. Once the women of the sample met the objective and subjective criteria, I moved into the area of recidivism, with recidivism being defined as "the reversion of an individual to criminal behavior after he or she has been convicted of a prior offense, sentenced, and (presumably) corrected."[40] These criteria were incorporated because I wanted to include women who had desisted after having a history of offending. Of the twenty-eight women, seven of them reported they had more than two to three years of crime-free behavior despite their multiple previous offenses. Given this information by the seven women, I felt I had to include an operational approach in the project to correlate recidivism as it relates to the disparities and desistance from crime.

---

[39] Patrick A. Langan and David J. Levin, *Recidivism of Prisoners Released in 1994* (Washington, DC: US Department of Justice, Bureau of Justice Statistics, 2002).

[40] Michael D. Maltz, *Recidivism* (Orlando: Academic Press, 1984).

Imprisonment has been used in the female population in a manner that often results in shorter sentences, which in turn compounds the high rates of return to prison (recidivism rates) for women entering prison for the first time. Among the thousands of women who are released from prison every year, recidivism is more frequent because they are left with no hope or safety to assist them in their survival and their fight against recidivism. The circumstances that await the female ex-offender make a tremendous impact on her likelihood of recidivism. It is for this reason that strategies must be called upon to address the disparities faced by women and the successful methods such women use to desist crime. Thus, for an examination that offered effective findings, in-depth interviews were performed and in-depth narratives were gathered to match women in the sample and review the reentry experiences of the matched sample of women ex-offenders who were in the process of desistance against those of women ex-offenders who were recidivists yet had been released once again. The sample was analyzed and insight was gleaned on the pathways women take to crime. It is found that recidivism is expressly high during the first year after release from prison with 44 percent of released prisoners being rearrested during that period.[41] Adding to this finding is the fact that female ex-offenders with prior offenses, a substance abuse history, and a limited education are more likely recidivate.[42] Subsequently, in order to offer a holistic view of successful reentry with desistance and disparities being the determining variables, recidivism had to be incorporated in this attempt to offer successful strategies for female ex-offenders exiting the prison system. The result of this holistic view, for the sample, provided a comparative analysis of current and former women offenders and gave the ability to heighten the understanding of the relationship between disparities, female ex-offender reentry, recidivism, and desistance. The women interviewed in this project made up a matched sample of former and current offenders. This allowed for the identification of the factors

---

[41] Langan and Levin, *Recidivism of Prisoners Released in 1994*.

[42] W. Reed Benedict and Lin Huff-Corzine, "Return to the Scene of the Punishment: Recidivism of Adult Male Property Offenders on Felony Probation, 1986–1989," *Journal of Research in Crime and Delinquency* 34 (1997): 237–52.

influencing recidivism, which helps in understanding the desistance process experienced by women who face the disparities of reentry into society.

## Data Collection

Data was retrieved from interview and narrative sources. The transitional home offered me time and allowed me to make appointments with women at their convenience. A set schedule was listed for women to sign up for passes and visitation privileges. These passes enabled the women to speak to me not only at the site of the transitional home. There were interviews conducted during lunches, recreational outings, and dinners. There were also passes that permitted outings to participate in church activities, at which time I incorporated my questions with the respondent's permission. At other times, I counseled women with substance abuse problems, family crises, educational problems, employment problems, and premarital problems. I also provided family counseling upon the release of female ex-offenders with their children and took notes for future reference. Counseling two women with their fiancés was a challenge, but it opened my eyes to the relational factors conflicting women who have been incarcerated for long periods of time. Many factors were discussed that affect the variables associated with successful reentry as it relates to the disparities, desistance, and recidivism. I did not have access to official sentencing records for the women in my sample; however, my reliance was on my interaction with them, my interview/narrative note collection, and the statistical information I obtained to contextualize the qualitative component of the research. Name, race, age, and marital status was provided to me directly from the women; however, the sentencing county was not released unless the female felt comfortable enough to provide it. Criminal histories were also afforded me from each woman who felt free enough to share her criminal history with me. Additional data was provided to me by the women that included the offense that had led to their last incarceration, the length of their prison sentence, the date they were last released from prison, the date of their upcoming release, and the county in which they would be paroled. Lastly, to complete my findings, additional information was provided about the sample that included the reasons for their parole revocation, the reason for their being sent back to prison, and the reason for any additional charges along with the new charges.

In a quest to utilize the most effective guide for the project at hand, I did research to retrieve the best instrument. It was found that Leverentz's guide fit the criteria needed.[43] In addition, Maruna's guide offered assistance in this endeavor.[44] For an in-depth interview, I modified some questions slightly and added some questions to gather information about the women's involvement in crime, their relational concerns and experience with family and friends, and the impact incarceration had had on them and their families. There were also in-depth interview questions that addressed premarital and marital issues facing female ex-offenders reentering society. As I developed the questions from my two literary guides, I examined the reason for conducting the interviews and created my questions in such a way as to direct the conversation toward the topics and issues I wanted to learn about. Questions were also carefully considered in order to provide guidance on what to do or say subsequent to the interviewee's answer to the last question. Because the interview guide developed served as my data-collection plan, it was important to base questions on what I had already found through research and on what I had gathered from my interaction with the women over the course of the eight years I had been in their lives as a mentor/sponsor. As an active participant in their reentry process, I had a prior observer's perspective on many of the situations they were facing. What I knew already was that most of the women who had been convicted of drug-related offenses were African Americans. Another insight was that after release from prison, female ex-offenders viewed their relationships

---

[43] Andrea Leverentz, *People, Places, and Things: The Social Process of Reentry for Female Ex-Offenders* (Washington, DC: National Institute of Justice, 2006).
[44] Shadd Maruna, *Making Good: How Ex-Convicts Reform and Rebuild Their Lives* (Washington, DC: American Psychological Association, 2001).

with families as important sources of both support and stress. Because of the limitation placed on intimate relationships, not many women had romantic relationships with individuals of the opposite sex, except those who had no history of drug use or offending. Another insight gathered from conversation was the restraint used by women in deciding whether or not to enter romantic relationships, because of their commitment to rehabilitation. Many were guided in this manner by support groups such as Alcoholics Anonymous and Narcotics Anonymous. Others restrained themselves because of the detrimental effects of relationships on their reentry. Most women believed in the importance of establishing their independence and the ability to achieve rehabilitative success before seeking a romance. Questions also had to be developed that addressed the sensitive issue of same-sex relationships since such proclivity was very evident in my interaction with the women. At the time interviews began, I had already developed relationships with all the women. Their condition ranged from being freshly out of prison to having been out of prison for between a few weeks and three years. The women were interviewed four times over the course of six months. However, many of the responses and findings stemmed from interaction with the women prior to the interviews. This assisted me in the in-depth portion of the interview because it allowed me to give the women more room to expound on their previous conversations and narratives with me and to describe their perceptions of the challenges they faced as they transitioned from prison to the community.

Although the interview guide contained open-ended questions, an important fact for me to remember was that the interviews were social occasions. The social interaction that occurs during an interview could not be avoided, especially given the previous relationship I'd developed with each woman prior to the project. Thus, even though the interviewee would want to put her best foot forward, they all felt free to discuss almost anything with me. However, for those just initiating a relationship with me, sensitive issues were not divulged as openly. Despite this possibility, everything during the interview conveyed a social message to the interviewees. Therefore, how I dressed, my mannerisms, my nonverbal cues, and my religious stance on issues such as same-sex relationships had to be carefully conveyed. Most perceived me as someone who had been where they were now and who understood the disparities they faced, along with the inability to desist from crime at one point, but who now possessed the ability to reenter society as a productive member of society, giving back what was so freely given to me.

The interview started with asking the women about their contact with law enforcement and their initial participation in crime. Information was then collected regarding their having been victims of crime, along with descriptions of what happened, why it happened, and how it happened. Though some did not want to describe their crime(s) in detail, the consequences of what they had done posed no problem for any of them. We then moved into the initial incarceration process and discussed what it looked like for them. Further questioning extracted information about what a day was like in prison, what resources were available, and what advantages and disadvantage were extracted from prison. Some advantages were given in the question, such as correctional and prerelease programs. The question then became whether they had participated in these programs and, if so, if they were helpful to them. If they were not helpful, why not? Questions were asked about relationships and how prison had affected those relationships.

A shift was then made in the type of question as the spotlight was placed on the reentry process. Upon release, what challenges had the women faced, and what type of anxiety had they felt as a result of being unsure of the future? Moving forward, information was taken of their employment status, their housing status, and their family status at the current time. Other questions included their recovery methods from substance abuse, sexual abuse, and others forms of abuse that may have affected their desistance from crime. Those who were professed repeat offenders were asked questions about their repeated convictions and their inability to desist crime. The final portion of the interview sought answers related to the women's goals, whether short term or long term. Also included was what agencies they would access and what kind of support system they had, because they needed help to accomplish their goals. As a result of the series of interviews, each woman seemed lifted and internally freer than before the interviews thanks to the opportunity to share her anxieties and frustration with someone who had been there and had survived successfully. The therapeutic value of one person helping another through her experience, strength, and hope is without parallel.

An analysis of the data collected reflected patterns of the sample finding. It included an analysis of how the respondents viewed and defined their lives. This was achieved using Strauss's way of thinking about and studying the social reality of the project presented.[45] Glaser and Strauss developed the grounded theory, which is a method that has been used extensively in the social science disciplines. "A grounded theory is one that is discovered, developed, and provisionally verified through systematic data collection and analysis of data pertaining to a particular phenomenon."[46] This method of data analysis required me to be sensitive theoretically while being well grounded in the technical literature. It was also necessary to be well-informed in terms of the personal and professional experience of the project. Thus, I found this analysis of data to be valuable in conducting empirical research and great for the use of qualitative techniques.

---

[45] Anslem L. Strauss, *Qualitative Analysis for Social Scientists* (Cambridge, MA: Cambridge University Press, 1987).

[46] A. L. Strauss and J. Corbin, *Basics of Qualitative Research: Techniques and Procedures for Developing Grounded Theory* (London: Sage, 1990, 1998).

# CHAPTER 5
# BIBLICAL RESPONSE

There is a wide array of challenges associated with the incarceration of women and their subsequent release. Now at a record high, the number of incarcerated women reflects that there will be continued growth in the future. Despite this fact, women make up a small minority of all who are incarcerated and reenter society from state correctional facilities. This is noteworthy when researching methods to ensure successful reentry. Just as noteworthy are the consequences associated with choices. It is for this reason a biblical response has to be given to the disparity and desistance variables associated with the reentry of the female ex-offender into society. When looking at the criminal justice system, it is also important to observe the underlying cause of crime, which is sin. It is important to support strategies and inquiries with the Word of God and what He has set up as an answer to the world's sin-sick state. Thus, multiple scriptures are introduced to offer knowledge from the Word of God. There are also scriptures supporting the need for the female ex-offender to put her trust in God. Coming from a biblical perspective, I believe that the only hope available for all parties seeking the answer to the reentry process of women into society lies in the One who came to set the captives free: Jesus Christ.

As a living testimony of the power of Jesus Christ, I was not able to live life on life's terms until I experienced a revelation of redemption through Him. No matter what I had done, what choices I had made, how determined I was, or how strong my will was to be free, I could find no deliverance until I found Him as my Savior. The Word of God became alive to me, and I began to trust and believe in what He said. Thus, it was not by my might, or my power, but by God's Spirit that I found power to overcome the wiles of the enemy. Connecting to my church and to a spiritual program for addiction gave me clarity and fortification to fight the good fight of faith. Today, I give back what was so freely given to me. My life is devoted to women in crisis, along with their children. Presently, my focus is on opening a transitional home where women in crisis can find support, encouragement, and a visual testimonial of what God has done in my life.

God's Word in Isaiah 61:1 claims, "The Spirit of the Lord God is upon me, because the Lord has anointed me to bring good news to the poor; he has sent me to bind up the brokenhearted, to proclaim liberty to the captives, and the opening of the prison to those who are bound" (ESV). Therefore, the hope and justification needed for the woman who accepts Jesus Christ as Lord and Savior of her life bring about faith. This faith allows her to face the disparities associated with her situation and to accept the consequences of her criminal past with positive strategies. Acceptance, not denial, is the answer to many of the problems encountered by a woman ex-offender because there are penalties associated with criminal actions that must be paid. Thank God for Jesus Christ, who paid the price for sin and presents us as righteous before God through His blood if one accepts Him as Lord and Savior. As a result of living a life for Him, the female ex-offender must adhere to the Word of God and accept His response to her situation.

The first concept to support a biblical response stems from Romans 13:1–5. The scripture points out the need to submit to the governing authorities:

> Let everyone be subject to the governing authorities, for there is no authority except that which God has established. The authorities that exist have been established by God. Consequently, whoever rebels against the authority is rebelling against what God has instituted, and those who do so will bring judgment on themselves. For rulers hold no terror for those who do right, but for those who do wrong. Do you want to be free from fear of the one in authority? Then do what is right and you will be commended. For the one in

> authority is God's servant for your good. But if you do wrong, be afraid, for rulers do not bear the sword for no reason. They are God's servants, agents of wrath to bring punishment on the wrongdoer. Therefore, it is necessary to submit to the authorities, not only because of possible punishment but also as a matter of conscience.

In this text, it is important for the female ex-offender to know that hope in a future is only found in God's plan for her. God's plans are to add to her hope, not take away from it. He has a future mapped out for her if she would accept Him as her Lord. "'For I know the plans I have for you,' declares the Lord, 'plans to prosper you and not to harm you, plans to give you hope and a future'" (Jeremiah 29:11). Submitting to authorities, as mentioned by Paul in Romans 13, is essential for those reentering society because the authority of the land comes from God. As a believer, which is the hope for those seeking successful entry, I must note that there is no authority except that which comes from God. Therefore, the reason for submission to authority, whether it is comfortable or not, is to honor God and to avoid any punishment or discipline by Him for not doing so. Rebelling against authority, repeating offenses, and engaging in criminal behavior is rebellion against authority. It then becomes rebellion against God and what He has instituted. There is judgment that is brought upon those who rebel against what God has instituted.

Adding to this concept is the scriptural text that reads as follows:

> Submit yourselves for the Lord's sake to every human authority: whether to the emperor, as the supreme authority, or to governors, who are sent by him to punish those who do wrong and to commend those who do right. For it is God's will that by doing good you should silence the ignorant talk of foolish people. Live as free people, but do not use your freedom as a cover-up for evil; live as God's slaves. Honor all people, love the brotherhood, fear God, honor the king. (1 Peter 2:13–17)

This scriptural text is important for the female ex-offender to understand. However, the first course of understanding is knowing that there is a full life promised to her as believers. Though she may have fallen short in the past, there is hope for the believer, no matter her past. God can move the mountains in her life and justify her by faith as a believer. Therefore, facing disparities as a female ex-offender and the urge not to desist from crime can be lifted through the power of God, which comes from a believer's trusting in God's power and His ability to move mountains / remove disparities. The second thing to understand about this scripture is that submission to authorities is done for God's sake. Submitting to the authorities, whether on parole, in a transition home, or living in society with laws, demonstrates one's submission to God. It is though submission, following God's precepts during reentry, and faithfulness to God that the woman of God reentering society can prosper despite the disparities. Wisdom in finding favor and prosperity can be found in the decree which states, "Let love and faithfulness never leave you; bind them around your neck, write them on the tablet of your heart. Then you will win favor and a good name in the sight of God and man" (Proverbs 3:3–4). Once this is achieved, the ability to desist from criminal activities and to overcome the disparities that go hand in hand with reentry into society can be developed. This concept must be instilled in the women exiting prison before strategic measures can be put in place for successful reentry. There must be a change in their lives that awakens the spirit inside them.

**The Response of the World**

Many debates have been conducted among believers that explore the issue of forgiveness and what it means for those convicted of criminal offenses. The consensus is that since Christ came for the forgiveness of the sin of humankind, human beings should forgive the offender and also relinquish the criminal offenses enacted by him or her. Though it is true that humankind is justified by faith, there are consequences for sin. Because of Jesus Christ, our righteousness, which is as filthy rags, is how God sees us if we have Him as our Savior. However, we are the righteousness of God through Jesus Christ. "For God made Christ, who never sinned, to be the offering for our sin, so that we could be made right with God through Christ" (2 Corinthians 5:21 NLT). In lieu of this, many critics suggest that Christians cannot support capital punishment or the death penalty because it would be contradictory to Christ's example. They believe that Jesus Christ came to save humankind and offer full forgiveness and freedom.

However, intermingling the stance of the Bible and that of society when seeking strategic solutions to a criminal's reentry is a complex process. The initial observation of the two, Christianity and politics, must be viewed through the prism of the Word of God to get a full understanding of the need for separation. Jesus explained to His disciples that there is a definite separation when it comes to the kingdoms of this world and His kingdom. In John 18:36, Jesus stated, "My kingdom is not of this world: if my kingdom were of this world, then would my servants fight, that I should not be delivered to the Jews: but now is my kingdom not from hence" (KJV). The kingdom of Christ is heavenly, and it was established seeking the reconciliation of the sinner to God. This differs from the civil and world governments of the earth, which seek power and supremacy.

In 2 Corinthians 5:20, Paul teaches more about the separation of church and state. He refers to Christians as ambassadors who represent the kingdom of God. The definition of an ambassador is "one who represents a country to another country." An ambassador also seeks the best for the welfare of those he represents as his own and does not become involved in the government of the other country. This is why the Christian ambassador does not become involved in the affairs of earthly governments. However, he does represent the heavenly kingdom to the world. For the female ex-offender, she is in this world but is not of this world (John 17:16). Therefore, she believes, as do those who seek strategies for her successful reentry, that her work is spiritual, not political. As for those seeking to aid her in whatever capacity available, their responsibility is to help her assess allegiance to the heavenly kingdom of Christ. In Isaiah 42:6–7, the Word of God reads, "I, the Lord, have called you in righteousness; I will take hold of your hand. I will keep you and will make you to be a covenant for the people and a light for the Gentiles, to open eyes that are blind, to free captives from prison and to release from the dungeon those who sit in darkness." If this is the case, then the response of the Christian believer should be one of strategically guiding the female ex-offender into the type of freedom that comes only from God. Following the example of Jesus is the answer to the controversy associated with the world response versus the Christian response.

Jesus gave a living testimonial of how criminals should be treated in Matthew 2:12: "It is not the healthy who need a doctor, but the sick. I have not come to call the righteous, but sinners" (Mark 2:17). Though He was berated for eating with tax collectors and sinners, He did not change His response to their situation. Thus, from Jesus's example, Christians are to love their brothers and sisters regardless of their sins. In 1 Peter 4:8, the Word of God says, "Above all, love each other deeply, because love covers over a multitude of sins." If this is the case, then the Christian believer is commanded to love despite others' shortcomings. Though this seems complex, there is something to the cliché' that says, "Love the sinner; hate the sin." Scripture does not include this saying; however, it does say, "Be merciful to those who doubt; save others by snatching them from the fire; to others show mercy, mixed with fear— hating even the clothing stained by corrupted flesh" (Jude 1:2–23). Thus, as believers, our lives should reflect this type of mercy for the sinner and a healthy hatred of sin and its effects. Jesus's life exhibited this mentality and active love alike. This can be seen in His dealings with those for whom others felt contempt because of their immorality.

In the days when Christ walked the earth, tax collectors were viewed with contempt and were place in a different category from the rest of the sinners. They were despised and thought of as treacherous and even criminal. However, Jesus's response to them was to break bread with them, eat with them, and even minister to them as He spent time in their company. Even with what they had done, He did not overlook them, though He also did not overlook what they had done. They had become immoral through sin sickness; however, He offered forgiveness, kind words, friendship, and salvation. It is this kind of response that is needed to counter the response of the world.

But the world does not provide such a response. The state counters the believers in their beliefs, in that the responsibility of the state is a sort of "out of sight, out of mind" concept. However, this stance of "out of sight, out of mind" is not an attitudinal option for Christians. The Christian believer must emphasize the elements of forgiveness, justice, repentance, and restoration. Therefore, the "locking up prisoners and throwing away the key" mentality of the world is debunked by the Christian believer's practice. This makes the responsibilities of the state quite different from those of individual believers. As observed in previous scriptures cited, God has appointed the state to maintain justice and punish wrongdoers. It has been established by God that humankind must submit to authority. There is an obligation to enact punishment when crimes are committed.

With the rise in the incarceration of women in the United States comes a rise in the number of women reentering society. Almost seven hundred thousand inmates left state and federal prison in 2005, which averages approximately nineteen hundred per day.[47] This represented 12 percent, or ninety-three thousand, of those on parole supervision.[48] However, even though the female ex-offender has served her time, she still faces disparities and the consequences of her conviction. Drawing from the twenty-eight women interviewed, I found that imprisonment served a different function in biblical times than it does in modern liberal

---

[47] Paige M. Harrison and Allen J. Beck, *Prison and Jail Inmates at Midyear 2005* (Washington, DC: US Department of Justice, Bureau of Justice Statistics, 2006).
[48] L. E. Glaze and T. P. Bonczar, *Probation and Parole in the United States, 2006* (Washington, DC: US Department of Justice, Office of Justice Programs, Bureau of Justice Statistics, 2007).

democracies. During those times, society was also very different, with stronger community bonds and different types of punishment options available to authority. One noticeable difference was the location of prisons in the ancient world, usually underground dungeons, or empty cisterns or wells, or pits in ground. The prison was a dark and miserable place. Evidence of this is given in Jeremiah, when he was put in "a cistern house" for many days (Jeremiah 37:20). When he was released to be questioned, he begged to be released entirely and not put back for fear he would die. By way of contrast, today's modern prisons may appear to some as hotels in comparison to prisons in biblical times. Certainly our prisons are more humane in terms of physical treatment of inmates. But they are still a source of great suffering. Many prisons today, no matter their accommodations, are places where pain, hurt, and hurting people are seen. Oftentimes the inmates suffer to a degree well beyond what landed them in prison because of their being deprived of their freedom. There is also a loss of dignity, autonomy, and contact with others because of the long periods of isolation from loved ones and friends. It is no wonder incarceration is used as a form of punishment when these elements are inflicted on women. The definition of punishment is the delivery of pain. Thus, punitive pain is received when women are imprisoned, which in essence contradicts our humanity as believers. As believers, we know that we are made in the image of God as free creatures. Taking away freedom hits at the heart of our identity as Christians. However, we live in a world where punitive punishment is expected if offenses against the system and the lawmakers' rules are committed. Therefore, as believers, we live in the world but are not of the world. We must recognize that prison is a place of pain, but we should also recognize the necessity of laws and of the judicial system. In doing so, we recognize that God is in control and uses us as His ambassadors to carry the good news to those inside prison walls. Even more than this, we are expected to bring hope to those who have suffered from the hurt of imprisonment and who seek to reenter society with dignity, faith, and a sense of newfound freedom. The disparities facing women exiting prison are great; however, the hope found in God is even greater.

Inside the prison walls, preparation can be made for women through prerelease preparation and linking them to postrelease support. This is why it is essential for women to attend support groups inside prison and once they reenter society. It does not start when they leave prison. It must start inside, through the offering of prerelease programs. Some of these programs include parenting classes, drug classes, Narcotics Anonymous, Alcoholics Anonymous, domestic violence classes, high school equivalency certifications, and Bible study groups. There is also a need for cultural and linguistic support for those women who are of different ethnicities from the mainstream. Preparation is a must for women seeking successful reentry into society and successful desistance from crime. It is for this reason that the factors affecting success or failure for women when exiting prison must be examined.

# CHAPTER 6
# INTEGRATION FACTORS AFFECTING SUCCESS AND FAILURE

In the United States, there are approximately seven hundred thousand inmates reintegrating home. The challenge to this crucial situation must be addressed strategically because of the fact that this number represents almost 93 percent of all inmates who will be, sooner or later, released from prison.[49] The process of leaving prison and returning to society is known as reentry. This process can be difficult for women as former offenders. Their newfound freedom associated with reentry is coupled with multiple legal and practical barriers. These barriers, often seen as inequalities for female ex-offenders, create disparities or impediments to their successful reentry into society.

When speaking with the women interviewed for this project, most of them cited housing, stable employment, family reunification and responsibility, sobriety, and integration with positive support networks as some of the obstacles they experienced as after their release from prison. Trying to enter into traditional society as former inmates has challenged each of their lives as they seek the means to do it successfully. The definition of *integration*, according to O'Brien (2001, 23), is "the former inmate's acceptance of adult role responsibilities according to her capabilities (i.e., economic sufficiency, parenting), the individual's perceptions of acceptance by the community despite what is often a stigmatizing status, and the woman's sense of self-esteem or self-efficacy."[50] Research has been conducted to establish certain documented factors that result in successful outcomes for female ex-offenders. Richie listed some of the factors that lead to successful reintegration/reentry:

---

[49] Joan Petersilia, "Parole and Prisoner Reentry in the United States," in *Prisons, Crime, and Justice: A Review of Research of Research*, edited by Michael Tonry and Joan Petersilia (Chicago: University of Chicago Press, 1999).

[50] Patricia O'Brien, *Making It in the "Free World": Women in Transition from Prison* (Albany: State University of New York Press, 2001).

access to community resources, involvement in programs that focus on empowerment, social support, and the use of comprehensive services.[51]

Because the women interviewed in this project were multifaceted with issues including abuse (childhood and adult), substance addiction, family dysfunction, minimal education level, sporadic work history, and poor health care, I used a comprehensive tool as has been highlighted by researchers as a method to meet the needs of women ex-offenders specifically.[52] Though there is no homogeneous definition of successful reintegration, the women interviewed reflected many of the summarized findings of a national study on effective correctional programs for women offenders. Koons and his colleagues found that the most promising programs available for successful reentry of women address multiple treatment needs.[53] These programs are known as "wraparound services," and they allow women facing multiple needs to receive assistance in one area and receive intervention at the same time in another area that addresses their other needs.[54] As an approach that works specifically with female ex-offenders suffering from multiple disparities, barriers, and problems, the wraparound services have been accepted as a successful holistic approach to successful reentry.[55]

---

[51] Beth E. Richie, "Challenges Incarcerated Women Face as They Return to Their Communities: Findings from Life History Interviews," *Crime and Delinquency* 47 (2001): 368–89.

[52] James Austin, Barbara Bloom, and Trish Donahue, *Female Offenders in the Community: An Analysis of Innovative Strategies and Programs* (Washington, DC: National Institute of Correction, 1992).

[53] Barbara A. Koons, John D. Burrow, Merry Morash, and Tim Bynum, "Expert and Offender Perceptions of Program Elements Linked to Successful Outcomes for Incarcerated Women," *Crime and Delinquency* 43 (1997): 512–32.

[54] Beth G. Reed, "Drug Misuse and Dependency in Women: The Meaning and Implication of Being Considered a Special Population or Minority Group," *International Journal of Addictions* 20 (1985): 13–62.

[55] William Rhodes and Michael Gross, *Case Management Reduces Drug Use and Criminality among Drug-Involved Arrestees: An Experiment Study of an HIV Prevention Intervention* (Washington, DC: National Institute of Justice and National Institute of Drug Abuse, 1997).

Just as important to this comprehensive approach is the need to look at the community and the effect it has on female ex-offenders as they reenter society. Providing connections to community resources and alleviating negative factors from the social environment women are reentering can assist in successful reintegration.[56] How women survive transitioning from prison to community is strongly correlated to the connections provided through community resources. There are obstacles and disparities that must be eliminated upon the women's release. These include the following:

- reconnecting to home and family life, which entails recapturing legal and physical custody of children;
- meeting the daily needs of life that are basic, and securing affordable housing;
- obtaining secure employment with sufficient income to pay for living expenses, despite the limited job skills or experience possessed;
- overcoming the limited opportunities offered in the way of vocational training while incarcerated;
- severing ties and deciding to continue/discontinue relationships that are abusive (sexual/physical) or exploitative;
- desisting from crime by establishing new relational connections that fortify noncriminal attitudes and behaviors;
- meeting the standards of the varied conditions of a parole plan;
- abstaining from alcohol or drug addiction and living a sober life; and finally,
- enduring the stigma associated with women ex-prisoners by family, friends, potential employers, community members, and potential landlords.[57]

During the interviews conducted, questions were asked about the women's health status (physical and mental health), their history of

---

[56] Barbara E. Bloom, *The Empowered Manager: Positive Political Skills at Work* (San Francisco: Jossey-Bass, 1991).
[57] Ibid.

abuse, criminal background, substance addictions, alcohol addiction, prior treatment opportunities for abuse of alcohol and/or other drugs, custodial experiences, family relationships, and peer relationships. The questions were also focused on the effect of these things in their time before incarceration, during their incarceration, and after incarceration. Recalling the sample group of twenty-eight women, with seventeen being African American and eleven being Caucasian, we recall that the project for them included three phases of reentry with recidivism being the first factor looked at because six of the women interviewed had incurred a new offense, a law violation, or a technical violation within a period of two to three years following release from prison. Recidivism is defined as relapse, devolution, regression, or recession. For the purposes of this project, recidivism is considered the devolution into criminal behavior. Also for our purposes, it is important to know that a recidivist is a person who is released from prison and later commits another crime. This reoffender has committed an act such as a parole violation or a new burglary. Thus, the respondents interviewed were included in the recidivism sample if they were noted as having or reported as having involvement in criminal activity since their last release from prison. Those women reincarcerated for committing a technical violation were also included in the sample. A total of six women were included as recidivist individuals. There are different operational approaches when researching recidivism that utilize measurements drawing from a new arrest, a return to prison, or a violation of probation or parole conditions, or the time frame when the female ex-offender is rearrested and reconvicted or suffers revocation of her parole/probation.[58]

**Success in Reentry**

From the interviews conducted, direct observation, and participation in the lives of women exiting prison, I have found it to be beneficial to

---

[58] Candace Kruttschnitt, Rosemary Gartner, and Amy Miller, "Doing Her Own Time? Women's Responses to Prison in the Context of the Old and the New Penology," *Criminology* 38 (2000): 681–718.

empower women with skills and support through programs that meet their specific needs. This type of empowerment is considered effective community programming that hones coping skills and decision-making skills and expands the options available to the female ex-offender. The practices implemented in the empowerment of women helps develop "intrapersonal, interpersonal, and social power that enables [them] to make efficacious choices for everyday life."[59] Independence, the main focus of empowerment, leads to successful reintegration. This is accomplished through a series of spiritual developmental variables that allow women to evaluate their personal behavior, discover their need for change through positive role models, and give to others.[60] Because women exiting prison need a vision and purpose, their self-esteem and confidence levels have to be boosted. This is where social support comes in, which is defined as the "provision of affective and/or instrumental (or material) resources ... [through] intimate or confiding relationships."[61]

This important element of successful female ex-offenders is seen as key to their reentry into the community and into a traditional life. Therefore, connectivity with friends, family, and community, along with other previously severed or new relationships, can lead to a successful reentry process. According to Maidment, her study revealed that interpersonal relationships, along with support systems that are socially based, are crucial to women's success during the reentry stage.[62] It is also noted that women who are willing to extract support through their professional relationships, other recovering people, ex-offenders, and associates for support and skill development can decrease their overwhelming sense of powerlessness in coping with the challenges during different points in the transition.

---

[59] Patricia O'Brien, *Making It in the "Free World."*
[60] Tessa Hale, "Creating Visions and Achieving Goals: The Women in Community Service's Lifeskills Program," *Corrections Today*, accessed December 15, 2020, http://www.corrections.com/aca/cortoday/archives.html, 2001.
[61] Francis T. Cullen, John P. Wright, and Mitchell B. Chamlin, "Social Support and Social Reform: A Progressive Crime Control Agenda," *Crime and Delinquency* 45 (1999): 188–207.
[62] Madonna R. Maidment, *Doing Time on the Outside: Deconstructing the Benevolent Community* (Toronto: University of Toronto Press, 2006).

## Success through Relationships

The bridge between the female ex-offender and the community, which can greatly affect successful reentry, is found in the individual's personal and social relationships. These relationships play a major role in the capacity to connect the female former offender to law-abiding citizens and legitimate institutions while providing her with a lawful identity and a connection to conventional society.[63] This project attempts to establish further evidence through research, interviews, and prior studies. To do so, examination of the factors that led formerly imprisoned females to successfully reintegrate into the community, along with the factors that resulted in reintegration failure for such women, will be determined.

The twenty-eight women interviewed gave their perceptions of the process of reentry/reintegration into the community from prison. As products of the state prison and its surrounding affiliated women's facilities, the women interviewed relayed that they had been steered toward a number of resources to successfully transition from prison to the community. This was done through the varied opportunities offered by the correctional center to cope outside the prison walls. Each of the women gave insight into the different elements of support she had received and the importance of such support in her life. One of the specific support systems available to the women was that made up of adult family members and children. Another important source of support was finding employment, which all the women reported was provided through access to programs inside and outside of prison during imprisonment and postimprisonment, saying that this helped facilitate their reentry efforts.

The support of family is an important element to the reentry of female former offenders into society. More specifically, of the twenty-eight

---

[63] Gordon Bazemore and Carsten Erbe, "Reintegration and Restorative Justice: Towards a Theory and Practice of Informal Social Control and Support," in *After Crime and Punishment: Pathways to Offender Reintegration*, edited by Shadd Maruna and Russ Immarigeon (Portland, OR: Willan, 2004).

female ex-offenders interviewed in the sample, approximately 80 percent highlighted the importance of receiving family support. They expressed how much this helped them to feel at ease in their traditional lives. This pattern was particularly common among seventeen African Americans in the sample. Of the eleven Caucasian females, two of them emphasized how important it was to have positive family support. For example, Betty, a forty-two-year-old Caucasian female, stated that her crime involved protecting her daughters. She was doing a life sentence that had been reduced to seven years. In preparing to be released from the transitional home in March of 2017, she was looking forward to bringing her daughters into her home. Recently she had lost her father and was wearied by not having been there for her family. However, her ties with her family and the support of her daughters had helped her make it through imprisonment and the transitional home, and likely would help her with her upcoming reentry into the community. Her positive family support was mentioned frequently, and her hope of reconnecting had given her the motivation to seek community support while still in the transitional home.

On the flip side, one of the African American females interviewed stated that her family had always been there for her. From providing financial support to helping to care for her children, they had kept her connected to her family. Upon her release from the transitional home, she resided with her mother, who had flown down from Connecticut and acquired a home for her and her children. Once she had reentered the community, she utilized the employment opportunities afforded her at the transitional home and began working in an area for which she had gained a certificate.

Inside the walls of the state prison and especially in the transitional home, the women are given the opportunity to acquire trades and certification for advanced career opportunities. In any case, the African American female connected with her family and began to be the primary provider with a trade in radio broadcasting. Most of the women who had been released shared that their families had stepped in when they reentered the community and helped them by taking them where they needed to go, taking care of their children, buying food and clothes, and giving them money for other essentials.

Just as important to the women was the spiritual and emotional support they received from family and church affiliation. The greatest obstacle for the women with children was in overcoming the feeling of guilt and shame when reentering the lives of their children. Therefore, one of the key elements for the successful reentry of these women was the emotional support received from their children. When one female in particular was interviewed, she stated that her greatest fan was her son. She was in prison when she initially got involved in recovery. Her son, sensing the importance of this in her life, began attending Al-Anon meetings to further assist her in her recovery from her substance abuse; to assist himself in his recovery from her substance abuse; and to assist the two of them in their recovery together upon his mother's reentry into the community. When she exited the transitional home, her son was at the airport in New York to meet her with roses and candy. Today, they both attend open meetings of Narcotics Anonymous, where he can support her and learn more about what she deals with. This type of affirmation from children is closely tied to reintegration/reentry success.

**Success through the Community**

There are multiple factors that determine the success of female ex-offenders reentering the community. Therefore, there is a need for multiple community-based programs. One such program is Narcotic Anonymous (NA). For those women reentering the community with substance abuse issues, NA offers a community-based setting through an association that provides a recovery process. The women are provided a support network where other members of the program share their successes and challenges in overcoming active addiction and living drug-free lives. The women interviewed in this project shared with me that this support group, along with other sister support groups of its kind in the community (e.g., Alcoholics Anonymous [AA], Overeaters Anonymous [OA], and Gamblers Anonymous [GA]), gives them strength and hope for living productive lives through the application of the twelve steps. Oftentimes, these twelve-step programs are offered during imprisonment and prerelease. The women interviewed shared the positive impact NA had made on their lives both inside and outside prison. Though one would think substance abuse would not be an issue for the women during their incarceration period, four of the women interviewed shared how accessible drugs were in prison and how important NA was to them when attempting to abstain from drug use behind bars. The most common program of this kind is known DART (Drug Awareness and Recovery Team). As a treatment program for recovering alcoholics and addicts, DART provides inmates who have problems with alcohol or other drugs an opportunity to engage in treatment and recovery. The criteria for participation are that the female offender be an inmate in medium or minimum custody and have a documented history of problems related to alcohol or other drugs. The women must also have a diagnosed alcohol or drug problem with a Substance Abuse Subtle Screening Inventory (SASSI) test score of 3–5. The women must also have been recommended by the court and must meet every criterion for the program. According to the program's operational guide, it is intended to do the following:

1. Introduce the treatment process.
2. Break through denial and achieve admission to and ownership of the problem.
3. Develop a recovery plan and a self-evaluation.
4. Transition from treatment to recovery and relapse prevention.[64]

The women represented in this project included twenty recovering addicts/alcoholics. Twelve of the women, including the two who had been released from the transitional home into the community and relapsed

---

[64] North Carolina Division of Prisons, accessed March 1, 2017, http://www.doc.state.nc.us/DOP/Program/dart.htm.

into substance abuse, had experimented with drugs or alcohol while at the transitional home. One of these women actually had a urinalysis while staying at the transitional home and had been sent back to prison for "dirty" urine. This number also reflects nine women who had been released from the state prison and had gotten away with "picking up" a substance again and not being penalized for doing so. However, these nine women, who were now involved in successful recovery programs, were struggling, yet surviving with the help of the twelve-step programs offered in the community. Recalling that twelve women in the project were dealing with substance abuse, we may conclude that it is imperative for the female ex-offender to be supported in her recovery efforts before and after her release from prison. Though there were many disparities and barriers that factor into the successful reentry of the women interviewed, substance abuse rated high on the list.

One of the primary reasons these women were arrested was for drug offenses. Female offenders are more likely than men to test positive for drug use at the time of arrest.[65] They are also cited as regularly using drugs more often than male inmates.[66] Of the twenty women interviewed with substance abuse problems in this project, eighteen had attempted drug treatment on the outside one or more times. When asked what kept them from relapsing and becoming involved with criminal activity again, the women shared complex reasons. However, in order to examine the surrounding reasons, I had to examine the context of the women's entire personal lives. As I was doing this, the women revealed several reasons that were seen as negative factors leading to their substance abuse. These factors were extracted through examination of the women's histories of family physical and sexual abuse, adult victimization, eating disorders, anxiety, and depression. All of these issues contributed to the women's substance abuse.

---

[65] C. Mann, "Women of Color and the Criminal Justice System," in B. Price and N. Sokoloff, eds., *The Criminal Justice System and Women: Offenders, Victims, and Workers*, 2nd ed. (New York: McGraw-Hill, 1995), 118–35.

[66] T. L. Snell, *Women in Prison*, Report No. NCJ-145321 (Washington, DC: US Government Printing Office, 1994).

It is a well-known fact that substance abuse is the symptom of the problems facing women offenders. In order to address the problem, the root must be exposed, or else the attempt to offer treatment becomes fruitless. Drug and alcohol treatment often deals with the feelings associated with the contributing factors of abuse. Thus, when attempting to initiate drug or alcohol treatment, one must address the underlying reasons the women use drugs. This is essential is one wishes to have successful results. Along with this is the need to examine the current desistance, the disparities, and the barriers to reentering the community.

**Success through Secure Employment**

Examining success for female ex-offenders includes not only family support and community support but also support when attempting to secure employment. The women interviewed, as well as information acquired through research, revealed that the ability to find and secure a job was essential to the successful reentry of women into society. The research cited that 42 percent of women obtained employment with the help of former employers, family, and friends. Research also revealed this pattern represented in 70 percent of the African American women, whereas it reflected only 30 percent of white women.[67] During the interviews, one woman in particular claimed that her family had a position waiting for her when she was released, adding how optimistic she was about being stable in the area of employment. While she had support from family, which was essential for the terms of her parole in being moved to another state, other woman feared not being able to secure employment when being released to areas outside their parole jurisdiction. For them, this meant having to find a job other than the job they were presently working in. The reason for this was that in order to live at the transitional home, employment was mandatory. If their release relocated them to another state where family could support

---

[67] Priscilla E. Greenwood and Michael, S. Nikulin, *A Guide to Chi-Squared Testing*, Wiley Series in Probability and Statistics (Hoboken: Wiley-Interscience, 1996).

them, they would have to give up their present jobs. An option for more than 50 percent of the women in this project was to secure housing in the city where the transitional home was located and continue to work at their current places of employment. In order to support their children and themselves, having a steady job was crucial.

The interview brought out the benefit of family support in the area of employment security as women expressed the hope they had as a result of knowing they would not have to face this barrier. I asked one of the interviewees, Gale, how she had gotten set up with finding employment. She reported that her sister worked for an automotive body shop and that had been there for one year. As a result, she was able to get Gale a job doing administrative work. To date, Gale has been moved up in her position and was transferred to another location of the same company. Another interviewee, Sandy, stated that her mother was a supervisor at a restaurant and that she had a job for her there when she was released. Though it offered minimal hourly pay, it was a start. It was also important to note that some of the women who relocated were assisted by their present employers. Upon release, three of the women were offered jobs as a result of their supervisor's or company's referrals to companies connected to their organization. One of the interviewees, Betty, expressed her gratitude to her employer for not only transferring her within the company to her hometown but also helping her find housing. This came directly from the employer's owning houses for his business and formulating a positive relationship with Betty that inspired him to invest in her successful reentry into the community. Family and employment networks such as these, which are already established, are vital to the reintegration process because "strong social relations … represent social and psychological resources that individuals can draw on."[68] Other venues were accessed by the women, such as word of mouth among the women residing in the transitional home. The transitional

---

[68] John H. Laub, Robert J. Sampson, Ronald P. Corbett, and Jinney S. Smith, "The Public Policy Implications of a Life-Course Perspective on Crime," in *Crime and Public Policy*, edited by Hugh D. Barlow (Oxford: Westview Press, 1995).

home is a place where women live and learn together how to adjust to the disparities, barriers, and desistance outside the walls of prison. Social capital, according to Portes, is the ability to secure employment, along with other beneficial assets, by way of being a member in social networks.[69] However, most of the interviewees lacked social capital given that social capital is based partly on one's position within the social structure.[70] It is found that women in the labor force possess fewer social ties than those outside it.[71] Thus, female ex-offenders have less access to the social networks necessary to gaining employment.

Securing employment provides the answer to many of the barriers faced by women reentering society. It also increases the likelihood of desistance from crime, while also helping to bridge the gap in the disparities that affect reintegration. It serves a multipurpose role in that it opens the door to social relations, increases social capital, provides economic stability and benefits, and gives the female ex-offender a sense of self-worth and status in the community.[72]

---

[69] V. Alejandro, "Social Capital: Its Origins and Applications in Modern Sociology," *Annual Review of Sociology* 24 (1998): 1–24.
[70] Nan Lin, "Inequality in Social Capital," *Contemporary Sociology* 29 (2000): 785–95.
[71] Ibid.
[72] James S. Coleman, "Social Capital in the Creation of Human Capital," *American Journal of Sociology* 94 (1998): 95–120.

# Chapter 7
# Abstaining from Crime Equals Desistance

To address abstinence from crime, it is essential to explore the findings revealing that women in prison have poor work histories and a low level of education. This makes it difficult to find a job in that they have no high school education. It is almost impossible for them to support themselves and their children by working a minimum wage job. In essence, education and occupational skills are valuable commodities to the female ex-offender. Self-worth and self-esteem are built when programs are offered that assist female ex-offenders in these areas. Abstaining from crime (desistance) is positively affected with the help of certificate programs, GED programs, and college courses offered inside and outside the prison walls. Through these programs, the women develop a sense of accomplishment. Such programs also provide answers to prospective employers who initially see an ex-offender as one who promises to bring little value to the company. However, through the help of these programs, some of the initial interview questions are answered with acceptable answers. Desistance can also be enhanced through programs such as vocational rehabilitation and job placement incentives, but the type of training offered to women in prison "does not necessarily assist women offenders in obtaining meaningful and financially rewarding work."[73]

## Therapeutic Approaches

Desistance begins with abstaining from crime. However, for the women interviewed, there needs to be a therapeutic approach to address the existing risk needs responsivity. This approach would work to bring

---

[73] M. L. Prendergast, J. Wellisch, and G. P. Falkin, "Assessment of and Services for Substance-Abusing Women Offenders in Community and Correctional Settings," *The Prison Journal* 75 (1995): 242.

about change in the female ex-offenders and support them in their efforts to desist from crime. The therapeutic approach is backed by research that stresses six central themes that should be utilized in rehabilitation programs and practice.[74] These are as follows:

- Intervention must accommodate and exploit issues of identity and diversity.
- Hope should be the key element to developing, motivating, and maintaining positive results from those working with female ex-offenders.
- Relationships between workers and offenders, as well as those between offenders and those who matter to them, are important.
- Rehabilitation can be supported by considering the ex-offender's strengths and resources, which include personal strengths and resources, along with the strengths and resources of those in their social networks.
- Interventions are meant to encourage and respect self-determination.
- The focus must be on working *with* offenders, not *on* them.
- Through intervention, human capital and social capital should be worked on.

A therapeutic approach should implement these principles, which ultimately will lead to behavioral changes. Changes are brought about through the facilitating of multiple coordinated services that support the female ex-offender. Some of these services focus on personal development, vocational skill building, and counseling. Therapeutic programs that work with women in prison have been noted as offering a type of philosophy that produces a more effective outcome than those with a punitive- and control-focused philosophy.[75] It is also important to note that this type of approach necessitates strengthened physical

---

[74] F. McNeill, "Four Forms of 'Offender' Rehabilitation: Towards an Interdisciplinary Perspective," *Legal and Criminological Psychology* (2012): 1–19.

[75] M. Lipsey, J. Howell, M. Kelly, G. Chapman, and D. Carver, *Improving the Effectiveness of Juvenile Justice Programs* (Washington, DC: Centre for Juvenile Justice Reform, 2010).

health, improved mental health, and education and training support. To date, there are programs and practices offered in prisons that provide this type of approach, which is significantly different from the normal practices offered in women's correctional facilities.

Some prisons use a "therapeutic communities" model, which can be seen operating in several prison systems worldwide. This model mimics features found in independent living units and focuses on the peer support approach. The definition of a therapeutic community is a group-based approach that is participative and tailored for long-term residency. The residents include both clients and therapists living together. An example of a therapeutic community is the transitional home. However, more express and specific therapeutic communities can be found in the correctional facilities across the country that focus on achieving behavioral change through several small communities of prisoners living together in units and undertaking a therapeutic program. The transitional home features elements of the program, which includes prisoners having greater responsibilities in running the facility and which offers greater therapeutic involvement by staff with increased interactions with family and others outside the prison community.[76]

While the therapeutic approach is a proven factor in promoting desistance from crime, there are empirical elements that assist in promoting desistance as well. A jail exit survey is an excellent tool for gauging how to improve the community response to women ex-offenders. This survey has been found to be effective in data collection, which is a tool for painting a picture of the characteristics of women offenders. With this tool, policy makers can better understand their systems and become more equipped to modify assessment protocols, decision criteria, and/or correctional facility programs to achieve their goals more cost-effectively. Experiences of several jurisdictions have shown how jail exit surveys can inform policy changes to achieve better

---

[76] P. Bennett and R. Shuker, "Improving Prisoner-Staff Relationships: Exporting Grendon's Good Practice," *Howard Journal of Criminal Justice* (2010): 491–502.

outcomes for the women and the system. These jurisdictions have developed sound information on current arrest, pretrial detention, and sentencing practices as they affect women offenders and relate to their risk, needs, and life circumstances. An analysis of the results of many exit surveys brings about lessons learned. Because of this, policy makers are working on a number of policy issues affecting women offenders. These types of surveys help uncover the deep-rooted issues affecting women reentering society and offer strategic tools that can help in the development of policies and programs geared toward desistance intervention. One last survey to consider is a prison rehabilitation survey. This survey is meant for the women to express their views, formally or officially, of their prison experiences in detail in order to ascertain their condition. The survey offered in this project was given to the women interviewed, and the responses were meant to give a brief overview of what prison rehabilitation meant to them after they had experienced it. One question in particular brought mixed emotions and offered a look into the women's desire to desist crime. It was "Do you believe that the sentencing is fair for the crimes that have been committed?"

The majority of the twenty-eight women said no. They felt that they had committed their crimes either in self-defense or to protect their children. Eight women felt that they had not committed a crime, saying that, instead, they had a bad habit but were not bad people. For these women, substance abuse is what had placed them behind the prison walls. The remaining women had committed crimes such as embezzlement, robbery, or violent acts against others. They felt they deserved to be penalized. Many were grateful for the limited amount of time they had received, in contrast to the time they could have received. All in all, desistance was inspired by the sentencing the women had received. None of them wanted ever to have their freedom taken away again for any reason.

This leads up to the next question that will be elaborated on: "Do you think that human rights influence the way prisons rehabilitate people?" The answer to this was interesting because each woman felt her human rights had been violated in one way or another. Despite the liberty they all experienced when leaving jails where there were no outside/outdoor privileges, they still felt they had been cut off from society and suffered the negative ramifications imputed on others. Whether they were a contributing factor in a violation of another inmate or not, all had to suffer administrative sanctions. This answers to this question also reflected the desire of the women to abstain from crime so as not to have their human rights violated again.

Each element mentioned above helps in obtaining and maintaining abstinence from crime. In order to desist, there has to be a motivator. In order to motivate, there must be practical strategies in place. In order to have practical strategies, female ex-offenders and the community must work together. Freedom is not free. It must be worked at and behaviors have to be changed. Change is necessary for the female ex-offender. Without it, desistance after reentry cannot be achieved.

# CHAPTER 8
# RECOMMENDATIONS AND CONCLUSION

Through research, interviews, and empirical studies, the question of "What can be done to eliminate the dilemma of women upon reentering society after prison?" was examined. Though the women in this project seemed to have a good chance of successful reentry, the fact is that some of them returned a short time later. Despite the calls received from the state prison or the news of a woman returning to prison shortly after entering the transitional home, I fight to reduce this occurrence in as many lives as I can. No longer pondering the question, I set out on a journey to find answers that would bring successful results for those women reentering society facing disparities, barriers, and a surmountable number of variables that lead back to a life of crime. Instead of simply acknowledging the revolving door of the criminal justice system, I looked into the cause, why some of the women exiting could not or would not desist from crime. The answer came as I spoke with those who had left and those who were approaching exiting. Each female ex-offender seemed to think she was forced to reenter the community without being equipped, empowered, and/or encouraged through her social connections. They all feared leaving prison with policy and law dictating their futures and limiting their access to true liberty. As for the offenders who did not return to prison, their experiences were evaluated and findings were gathered to offer recommendations to those who seemed unable to desist from crime.

As I looked through the lenses afforded me by research and by looking into the backgrounds and experiences of female offenders who were preparing to leave prison and reenter society, I gathered as much detail as possible to provide recommendations. Throughout my research, I found that most studies of criminological research have been done on men, with little attention being paid to women. Thus, my first recommendation is to examine, in depth, the predictive validity of recidivism and desistance among women. This would help in assisting women who face the disparities, barriers, and challenges that accompany reentry into society with convictions, especially felony convictions. There is also a lack of research in the area of race-based variations when looking at women's postrelease experiences. The recommendation for this stems from the initial recommendation of more examination into women as opposed to men with a spotlight on the road that leads white women versus black women to crime. In each racial sector, it is evident from the study that there are certain factors that both assist and hinder successful reentry. There are also varied reasons for recidivating, which reflects specific methods and stimuli that can be used to desist crime. According to Peters and his colleagues, there are psychosocial challenges that incarcerated women face that must be examined in order to treat their psychiatric/psychological issues.[77] From this point of view, it is highly recommended that women offenders be provided in-house and community-based treatment programs that assess and provide support in the areas where female offenders suffer. These areas include sexual abuse, depression, psychotic disorders, substance abuse, posttraumatic stress disorder, panic, eating disorders, and other forms of mental illness.[78] There are also physical and environmental issues that need to be addressed when dealing with the disparities associated with female ex-offenders. These range from sexually transmitted diseases, high rates of homelessness, chronic illness such as HIV/AIDS, and unemployment.[79] Failure to diagnose these issues and offer treatment has resulted in three-fourths of female ex-offenders having a high probability of substance

---

[77] R. H. Peters, A. L. Strozier, M. R. Murrin, and W. D. Kearns, "Treatment of Substance-Abusing Jail Inmates: Examination of Gender Differences," *Journal of Substance Abuse Treatment* 14, no. 4 (1997): 339–49.

[78] Barbara Bloom, Barbara Owen, and Stephanie Covington, *Gender-Responsive Strategies for Women Offenders: A Summary of Research, Practice, and Guiding Principles for Women Offenders* (Washington, DC: US Department of Justice, National Institute of Corrections, 2005).

[79] R. L. McLean, J. Robarge, and S. G. Sherman, "Release from Jail: Moment of Crisis or Window of Opportunity for Female Detainees?" *Journal of Urban Health: Bulletin of the New York Academy of Medicine* 83, no. 3 (2006): 382–93.

abuse or dependence.[80] As recorded by Blitz through a survey conducted among women, women who receive treatment for addiction or mental health issues are noted as having a more stable employment history before incarceration. However, those who did not receive treatment in this area were less successful in regard to stable employment. Thus, Blitz concluded that access to treatment is an important key before and after incarceration. Therefore, the recommendation is for mandated treatment for women as the result of assessments performed inside prison and postrelease from prison to determine the plan of care that will be needed for successful reintegration into society.

Lastly, it is recommended that services be united to better assist the female ex-offender as she transitions from prison to community. This involves not only the ex-offender but also the family, potential employers, and friends who will be a part of her support system. This strategy offers various positive benefits in the area of desistance and community integration while giving the female ex-offender a sense of worth after exiting prison. Lastly, a spiritual awakening through spiritual support is essential to women who have been stigmatized by their prison experience. Knowing that God can and will "open doors that no man can close and close doors that no man can open" (Isaiah 22:22) builds faith and hope for the future. In order to desist crime, there must be a new way of thinking that ultimately comes from renewal of the mind for the female ex-offender. There must be a transformation away from doing the same old thing and expecting different results. Thus, scriptures are recommended that are honed into the heart and mind of the female ex-offender. Along with these scriptures should be a consistent fellowship of like-minded believers who can offer godly counsel in addition to conventional counseling. Since freedom is not free, it must be worked at. No longer being a slave to worldly desires and sinful/offensive acts, the female ex-offender chases after freedom through a relationship with her Creator. Then, and only then, can she say, "Who the Son sets free is free indeed" (John 8:36).

---

[80] P. Tonkin, J. Dickie, S. Alemagno, and W. Grove, "Women in Jail: 'Soft Skills' and Barriers to Employment," *Journal of Offender Rehabilitation* 38, no. 4 (2004): 51–71.

# BIBLIOGRAPHY

Austin, James, Barbara Bloom, and Trish Donahue. *Female Offenders in the Community: An Analysis of Innovative Strategies and Programs.* Washington, DC: National Institute of Correction, 1992.

Austin, James, and John Irwin. *It's about Time: America's Imprisonment Binge.* Belmont, CA: Wadsworth, 2001.

Bazemore, Gordon, and Carsten Erbe. "Reintegration and Restorative Justice: Towards a Theory and Practice of Informal Social Control and Support." In *After Crime and Punishment: Pathways to Offender Reintegration.* Edited by Shadd Maruna and Russ Immarigeon. Portland, OR: Willan, 2004.

Belknap, Joanne. *The Invisible Woman: Gender, Crime, and Justice.* Belmont, CA: Wadsworth, 1996.

Benedict, W. Reed, and Lin Huff-Corzine. "Return to the Scene of the Punishment: Recidivism of Adult Male Property Offenders on Felony Probation." *Journal of Research in Crime and Delinquency* 34 (1997): 237–52.

Bennett, P., and R. Shuker. "Improving Prisoner-Staff Relationships: Exporting Grendon's Good Practice." *Howard Journal of Criminal Justice* (2010): 491–502.

Blitz, C. L. "Predictors of Stable Employment among Female Inmates in New Jersey: Implications for Successful Reintegration." *Journal of Offender Rehabilitation* 43, no. 1 (2006): 1–22.

Bloom, Barbara E. *The Empowered Manager: Positive Political Skills at Work*. San Francisco: Jossey-Bass, 1991.

Bloom, Barbara, Barbara Owen, and Stephanie Covington. *Gender-Responsive Strategies for Women Offenders: A Summary of Research, Practice, and Guiding Principles for Women Offenders*. Washington, DC: US Department of Justice, National Institute of Corrections, 2005.

———. *Gender-Responsive Strategies: Research, Practice, and Guiding Principles for Women Offenders*. Washington, DC: National Institute of Corrections, 2003.

Bonta, James, Bessie Pang, and Suzanne Wallace-Capretta. "Predictors of Recidivism among Incarcerated Female Offenders." *The Prison Journal* 75 (1995): 277–94.

Britton, Dana M. "Feminism in Criminology: Engendering the Outlaw." *Annals of the American Academy of Political and Social Science* 571 (2000): 57–76.

Chesney-Lind, Meda. "Imprisoning Women: The Unintended Victims of Mass Imprisonment." In *Invisible Punishment: The Collateral Consequences of Mass Imprisonment*. New York: New Press, 2002.

Coleman, James S. "Social Capital in the Creation of Human Capital." *American Journal of Sociology* 94 (1988): 95–120.

Cullen, Francis T., John P. Wright, and Mitchell B. Chamlin. "Social Support and Social Reform: A Progressive Crime Control Agenda." *Crime and Delinquency* 45 (1999): 188–207.

Daly, Kathleen. "Gender, Crime, and Criminology." In *The Handbook of Crime and Justice*. Edited by Michael Tonry. Oxford: Oxford University Press, 1998.

Deschenes, Elizabeth P., Barbara Owen, and Jason Crow. *Recidivism among Female Prisoners: Secondary Analysis of the 1994 BJS Recidivism Data Set, Final Report.* Washington, DC: National Institute of Justice, 2007.

Gelsthorpe, L., G. Sharpe, and J. Roberts. *Provision for Women Offenders in the Community.* London: Fawcett Society, 2007.

Giordano, Peggy C., Stephen A. Cernkovich, and Jennifer L. Rudolph. "Gender, Crime, and Desistance: Toward a Theory of Cognitive Transformation." *American Journal of Society* 107 (2002): 990–1064.

Glaze, L. E., and T. P. Bonczar. *Probation and Parole in the United States.* Washington, DC: US Department of Justice, Office of Justice Programs, Bureau of Justice Statistics, 2007.

Greenfeld, Lawrence A., and Tracy L. Snell. *Women Offenders.* Washington, DC: Bureau of Justice Statistics, 1999.

Greenwood, Priscilla E., and Michael S. Nikulin. *A Guide to Chi-Squared Testing.* Wiley Series in Probability and Statistics. Hoboken: Wiley-Interscience, 1996.

Harrison, Paige M., and Allen J. Beck. *Prison and Jail Inmates at Midyear.* Washington, DC: US Department of Justice, Bureau of Justice Statistics, 2006.

———. *Prisoners in 2003.* Bureau of Justice Statistics Report. Washington, DC: US Department of Justice, 2004.

Hedderman, C. "The 'Criminogenic' Needs of Women Offenders: What Should a Programme for Women Focus On?" In *Women Who Offend.* Edited by G. McIver. London: Jessica Kingsley, 2004.

Heimer, Karen. "Changes in the Gender Gap in Crime and Women's Economic Marginalization." In *Criminal Justice 2000: The Nature of Crime, Continuity and Change.* Edited by Gary LaFree, vol. 1. Washington, DC: National Institute of Justice, 2000.

Holtfreter, Kristy L., Michael D. Reisig, and Merry Morash. "Poverty, State Capital, and Recidivism among Women Offenders." *Criminology and Public Policy* 3 (2004): 185–208.

Koons, Barbara A., John D. Burrow, Merry Morash, and Tim Bynum. "Expert and Offender Perceptions of Program Elements Linked to Successful Outcomes for Incarcerated Women." *Crime and Delinquency* 43 (1997): 512–32.

Kruttschnitt, Candace, Rosemary Gartner, and Amy Miller. "Doing Her Own Time? Women's Responses to Prison in the Context of the Old and the New Penology." *Criminology* 38 (2000): 681–718.

Langan, Patrick A., and David J. Levin. *Recidivism of Prisoners Released in 1994.* Washington, DC: US Department of Justice, Bureau of Justice Statistics, 2002.

Laub, John H., and Robert J. Sampson. *Shared Beginnings, Divergent Lives: Delinquent Boys to Age 70.* Cambridge, MA: Harvard University Press, 2003.

———. "Understanding Desistance from Crime." *Crime & Justice* 28 (2001): 1–58.

Laub, John H., Robert J. Sampson, Ronald P. Corbett, and Jinney S. Smith. "The Public Policy Implications of a Life-Course Perspective on Crime." In *Crime and Public Policy.* Edited by Hugh D. Barlow. Oxford: Westview Press, 1995.

Leverentz, Andrea. *People, Places, and Things: The Social Process of Reentry for Female Ex-Offenders*. Washington, DC: National Institute of Justice, 2006.

Lin, Nan. "Inequality in Social Capital." *Contemporary Sociology* 29 (2000): 785–95.

Lipsey, M., J. Howell, M. Kelly, G. Chapman, and D. Carver. *Improving the Effectiveness of Juvenile Justice Programs*. Washington, DC: Center for Juvenile Justice Reform, 2010.

Maidment, Madonna R. *Doing Time on the Outside: Deconstructing the Benevolent Community*. Toronto: University of Toronto Press, 2006.

Mallik-Kane, Kamala, and Christy A. Visher. *Health and Prisoner Reentry: How Physical, Mental, and Substance Abuse Conditions Shape the Process of Reintegration*. Washington, DC: Urban Institute, 2008.

Maltz, Michael D. *Recidivism*. Orlando: Academic Press, 1984.

Mann, C. "Women of Color and the Criminal Justice System." In *The Criminal Justice System and Women: Offenders, Victims, and Workers*. Edited by B. Price and N. Sokoloff, 2nd ed. New York: McGraw-Hill, 1995, 118–35.

Maruna, Shadd. *Making Good: How Ex-Convicts Reform and Rebuild Their Lives*. Washington, DC: American Psychological Association, 2001.

Massoglia, Michael, and Christopher Uggen. "Subjective Desistance and the Transition to Adulthood." *Journal of Contemporary Criminal Justice* 23 (2007): 90–103.

McLean, R. L., J. Robarge, and S. G. Sherman. "Release from Jail: Moment of Crisis or Window of Opportunity for Female Detainees?" *Journal of Urban Health: Bulletin of the New York Academy of Medicine* 83, no. 3 (2006): 382–93.

McNeill, F. "Four Forms of 'Offender' Rehabilitation: Towards an Interdisciplinary Perspective." *Legal and Criminological Psychology* (2012): 1–19.

Miller, Jody. "The Status of Qualitative Research in Criminology." Paper presented at the National Science Foundation Workshop on Interdisciplinary Standards for Systematic Qualitative Research, Washington, DC, 2005.

Minton, T. D., and W. J. Sabol. *Jail Inmates at Midyear 2008—Statistical Tables.* Washington, DC: US Department of Justice, Office of Justice Programs, Bureau of Justice Statistics, 2009.

North Carolina Division of Prisons. Accessed March 1, 2017. http://www.doc.state.nc.us/DOP/Program/dart.htm.

O'Brien, Patricia. *Making It in the "Free World": Women in Transition from Prison.* Albany: State University of New York Press, 2001.

Peters, R. H., A. L. Strozier, M. R. Murrin, and W. D. Kearns. "Treatment of Substance-Abusing Jail Inmates: Examination of Gender Differences." *Journal of Substance Abuse Treatment* 14, no. 4 (1997): 339–49.

Petersilia, Joan. *Parole and Prisoner Reentry in the United States.* Chicago: University of Chicago Press, 1999.

Phillips, Llad, and Harold L. Votey. "Black Women, Economic Disadvantage, and Incentive to Crime." *American Economic Association Papers and Proceedings* 74 (1984): 293–97.

Portes, Alejandro. "Social Capital: Its Origins and Applications in Modern Sociology." *Annual Review of Sociology* 24 (1998): 1–24.

Prendergast, M. L., J. Wellisch, and G. P. Falkin. "Assessment of and Services for Substance-Abusing Women Offenders in Community and Correctional Settings." *The Prison Journal* 75 (1995): 242.

Reed, Beth G. "Drug Misuse and Dependency in Women: The Meaning and Implication of Being Considered a Special Population or Minority Group." *International Journal of Addictions* 20 (1985): 13–62.

Rhodes, William, and Michael Gross. *Case Management Reduces Drug Use and Criminality among Drug-Involved Arrestees: An Experiment Study of an HIV Prevention Intervention.* Washington, DC: National Institute of Justice and National Institute of Drug Abuse, 1997.

Richie, Beth E. "Challenges Incarcerated Face as They Return to Their Communities: Findings from Life History Interviews." *Crime and Delinquency* 47 (2001): 368–89.

Schram, P. J., B. A. Koons-Witt, F. P. Williams III, and M. D. McShane. "Supervision Strategies and Approaches for Female Parolees: Examining the Link between Unmet Needs and Parole Outcome." *Crime & Delinquency* 52, no. 3 (2006): 450–71.

Sheehan, R. "Justice and Community for Women in Transition in Victoria, Australia." In *Women, Punishment and Social Justice: Human Rights and Penal Practices.* Edited by M. Malloch and G. McIvor. Oxford: Routledge, 2012.

Snell, T. L. *Women in Prison.* Report No. NCJ-145321. Washington, DC: US Government Printing Office, 1994.

Strauss, Anslem L. *Qualitative Analysis for Social Scientists.* Cambridge: Cambridge University Press, 1987.

Tonkin, P., J. Dickie, S. Alemagno, and W. Grove. "Women in Jail: 'Soft Skills' and Barriers to Employment." *Journal of Offender Rehabilitation* 38, no. 4 (2004): 51–71.

Travis, Jeremy. *But They All Come Back: Facing the Challenges of Prisoners Reentry.* Washington, DC: Urban Institute Press, 2005.

Ulmer, Jeffrey T. "Intermediate Sanctions: A Comparative Analysis of the Probability and Severity of Recidivism." *Sociological Inquiry* 71 (2001): 164–93.

Visher, Christy A., Pamela K. Lattimore, and Richard L. Linster. "Predicting the Recidivism of Serious Youthful Offenders Using Survival Models." *Criminology* 29 (1991): 329–66.

Visher, Christy A., and Jeremy Travis. "Transition from Prison to Community: Understanding Individual Pathways." *Annual Review of Sociology* 29 (2003): 89–113.

West, H. C., and W. J. Sabol. *Prison Inmates at Midyear 2008—Statistical Tables.* Washington, DC: US Department of Justice, Office of Justice Programs, Bureau of Justice Statistics, 2009.

Zarch, R., and G. Schneider. *The Jewish Vocational Services Women Offender Reentry Collaborative—A Practitioner's "Blueprint" for Replication.* Cambridge, MA: Abt Associates, 2007.

Lightning Source UK Ltd.
Milton Keynes UK
UKHW011954141122
412210UK00011B/159/J